HAGOP KEVORKIAN SERIES ON NEAR EASTERN ART AND CIVILIZATION

The publication of this work has been aided by
a grant from the Hagop Kevorkian Fund.

IRANIAN CITIES

Heinz Gaube

New York · New York University Press · 1979

Copyright © 1978 by New York University

Library of Congress Cataloging in Publication Data

Gaube, Heinz.
   Iranian cities.

   (Hagop Kevorkian series on Near Eastern art and civilization)
   Includes bibliographical references.
   1. Cities and towns—Iran. 2. Cities and towns,
Islamic—Iran. 3. Herat, Afghanistan. 4. Iran—
Social conditions. I. Title. II. Series.
HT147.I6G38   301.36′3′0955   77-25748
ISBN 0-8147-2971-1

Almost all illustrations are the author's photographs or drawings. Sources of the other illustrations are as follows. Fig. 5: C. Braun; *Tehran, Marrakesch und Madrid* (1974); Figs. 7-10: E. Wirth; *Die orientalische Stadt* (1975); Fig. 14: J. Sauvaget; *Alep* (1941); Fig. 15: J. Sauvaget; *Esquisse d'une histoire de la ville de Damas* (1934); Figs 21, 22, and 32: O.v. Niedermayer; *Afghanistan* (1924); Fig. 25: H. Gaube and E. Wirth; *Der Bazar von Isfahan* (1978); Figs. 48, 50, 51, 52, 57, and 61: H. Gaube and E. Wirth; *Der Bazar von Isfahan* (original field map); Fig. 60: TAVO-map A IX, 9.4, *Der Bazar von Isfahan;* Figs. 62 and 63: E. Ehlers; *Die Stadt Bam und ihr Oasen-Umland* (1975); Figures 17 and 18 are published by permission of the Oriental Institute of the University of Chicago.

Manufactured in the United States of America

Contents

Preface

From almost everyone the phrase "Iranian cities" evokes certain feelings, images, or memories. Some might think of the proverbial gardens of Shiraz, fading away little by little; others of Isfahan, the radiant capital of the Safavid state and today one of Iran's most important industrial cities; and still others of Tehran, which in the course of the past few decades has developed from a sleepy capital into a megalopolis.

All these are aspects of the "Iranian city," which is today undergoing a dramatic change. The process of westernization is rapidly gaining ground, swallowing up some things worth preserving as well as others not worth holding onto. Thus, even an Islamicist and historian, like the author of the following pages, when writing about Iranian cities, cannot simply revel in the seemingly sunny fields of times long past.

As a consequence, this study begins with a brief look at two modern Iranian cities, Tehran and Malayer, and uses them as a starting point for a voyage back to more remote times. Herat, Isfahan, and Bam, our other examples, are cities of different sizes, situated in the east, the west, and the south of historical Iran and flourish today as they did in the Middle Ages. Studying each of them under different aspects (and thus laying stress on different features) but using the same method in each case should fulfill the somewhat ambitious promise of the title "Iranian cities." The first chapter, "Origins," is introductory and supplementary to the following chapters. It provides a general foundation for the various topics, terms, and theories dealt with in this study.

Needless to say, any attempt at dealing with a topic as complex and as manifold as the city must confine itself to a few among many concerns. Thus, the questions treated here are concerned with the *origins,* the *contours,* the *growth,* and the *functions* of both the individual components and the whole of the cities under consideration. I have chosen these because my own approach to research on the subject was along the lines of historical geography. It comprises philological inquiries and archeological analyses as well as an attempt to argue on geographical lines.

Whereas the consideration of the combination of literary and archeological evidence is characteristic of most of the books and articles I have published since the early seventies, my study of Iranian cities began with an introduction to a geographic outlook on the Iranian city (and on the oriental city as a whole) from Professor Eugen Wirth of Erlangen University. Under Professor Wirth's guidance a number of Ph.D. theses on oriental cities have been written since the late sixties, and his numerous contributions to the study of the oriental city and the bazaar have set new research standards. Many of the ideas presented here have resulted from my trips to the bazaars of Aleppo and Isfahan or from discussions which followed our common work there. Thus, there is no better place than here to thank Professor Wirth for all the help and incentive a younger scholar can receive from a senior one—and in my case—still receives.

I also wish to thank my friend Professor Francis E. Peters of New York University. Our travels and discussions in the Ghassānid lands, east of the Ḥaurān and other parts of the Syrian desert, brought about the materialization of the ideas laid down in this study. Together with Professor Peters I thank all the other members of New York University's Hagop Kevorkian Center for Near Eastern Studies who made my stay in New York a lasting memory and to whose discussions I owe much.

Most of the new material evidence, maps, and plans presented here are by-products of my work for an institution I feel deeply committed to, the Sonderforschungsbereich 19 of Tübingen University, more generally known as the *Tübinger Atlas des Vorderen Orients (TAVO)*. In the TAVO-project scholars of different disciplines are collaborating in producing an atlas of about 250 maps of the Near East, the first of which were recently published.

Heinz Gaube
Tübingen

Foreword

New York University is proud to present this second volume in the *Hagop Kevorkian Series on Near Eastern Art and Civilization*. This work, like the one which preceded it and the others which will follow, reflects a commitment to excellence that has characterized the Hagop Kevorkian Lecture Series from which this book has been developed, and also the commitment of the Hagop Kevorkian Fund to both the work of scholars and the dissemination of scholarship on the Near East.

The particular focus of the Hagop Kevorkian Lectures is on the study of art in the framework of civilization, or, stated differently, the study of civilization through art. We are delighted that the series has attracted the interest and participation of some of the world's foremost scholars. Forthcoming volumes will deal with the development of the Iranian mosque, the principles of Islamic art, and the representational art in Canaan. None of these volumes or lectures could have been possible without the steadfast support of the Kevorkian Fund.

New York University is much indebted to the Fund for its support over the years. Most of all, we appreciate the vision and confidence of the trustees which have enabled this University to become a national resource in Near Eastern Studies.

Peter J. Chelkowski, Director
Hagop Kevorkian Center
   for Near Eastern Studies
New York University

List of Illustrations

xiii

Introduction

Socrates, on one of his rare walks outside of Athens, was asked why he did not favor the countryside. He had never, he replied, learned anything from a tree. It was not a novel idea, this preference for human company over communion with nature or, from another perspective, for talking over plowing. (Men of earlier generations, not only in Greece but in Mesopotamia, Egypt and Iran, had expended a great deal of time and energy in rearranging nature so that it would not merely support life but would provide a suitable setting for some of the exchanges Socrates had in mind and many others he knew about but chose to ignore.)

The final version of that setting was the city where notables and the lesser urban bourgeoisie lived and associated within the security of stout walls and military guardians. Here were their temples, churches, and mosques, their palaces, bazaars, and schools. From the city extended the roads and seaways which enabled them to exchange goods and ideas with their urban fellows across regions and even empires. From the riches of imperial cities new urban settlements were founded and older ones enlarged and beautified. While some cities were born and grew, others died lingering deaths or were suddenly and brutally destroyed.

The city is a highly self-conscious institution. Like Socrates, the elites of preindustrial societies were relentlessly urban in their outlook. Even when forced to live in the countryside, they quite conveniently carried their environment with them, and they had at their disposition, and among their number, scribes, memorialists, and propagandists in every known medium of communication. The "men of the pen," as they were called in Islamic times, were not students of the city as such but they left behind in their chronicle of events worth remarking a rich collection of material touching upon almost every aspect of city life: the lives of prominent citizens; internal revolts, public festivals, executions, food prices and shortages; the size, shape and location of public buildings; how money and reputations were made and lost.

Had we to rely solely on such sources, we would have a tolerably complete picture of city life in the age before industrialization. But we can do better. It is possible to exhume the physical remains of dead cities and even to catch, in still-living urban organisms, the shape and rhythm of their preindustrial predecessors. This is a delicate task, this listening for old harmonies under newer sounds, of seeing yesterday's skeleton under today's flesh. The urban archeologist takes his easy pleasure in a place like Palmyra or Persepolis where he has leisure and leave to perform an autopsy on a corpse. No such satisfactions await him in Jerusalem, Damascus, Baghdad, or Herat where the city lives on. The anatomist's dream of vivisection has never been shared by its subjects.

But as Jean Sauvaget in the thirties and now Heinz Gaube in *Iranian Cities* brilliantly illustrate, the history of the living can be understood as well as that of the dead. With chronicles in hand, Gaube has walked the streets of Iran's cities in search of the outlines of their past, not merely their static but their evolutionary past. In some instances a moment of that past leaps easily to the eye, as even the most casual visitor to Isfahan can attest. Elsewhere, even in Isfahan, it lies artfully concealed behind and beneath reconstructed buildings and redrawn city streets. New urban planners are at work in the old cities of Iran, and Gaube has had to contest with them, as he has had to contest with older urban planners like Shah 'Abbās who reshaped *their* urban past.

It must be left to the reader to decide whether Gaube has won his race against Heraclitus and Shah 'Abbās' architects. These are formidable adversaries and no single historian or archeologist might hope to match them. But Heinz Gaube is both: a historian who has also been over every square foot of these cities with the keen eye of the urban geographer and an archeologist with considerable field experience who can read literary texts in the best orientalist traditions.

If there is an *intimacy* of knowledge in these pages, there is a *complexity* as well because cities are complex places to begin with and develop in complex ways. Their internal configurations are as intricate as the web of family relationships that were part of the mortar of urban life before modern times. Their wide thoroughfares and open places invite the urbanist to enter; once within, however, he is confronted with the maze of alleys that Gaube has so skillfully disentangled. The mosque is eminently accessible with its broad lines and open spaces. But for every mosque in these cities there were thousands of private places giving only blind walls to the street and masking their recesses to all but the most persistent enquirer. Studying cities requires some of the same virtues demanded of those who live in them: determination, perseverance, courage, and imagination. But Socrates was probably right, once again.

F. E. Peters
Hagop Kevorkian Center
  for Near Eastern Studies
New York University

IRANIAN CITIES

CHAPTER ONE

Origins

1. INTRODUCTION

More than 1300 years ago, the Arabs and, with them, Islam conquered Iran.[1] On the same soil where another 1200 years earlier the Achaemenid state, the first world empire in history, had originated, a new Irano-Islamic civilization began to grow. Its distinct achievements and characteristics bear witness to Iran's individuality in the framework of Islamic civilization. This individuality is, however, a product of an Irano-Semitic cultural exchange which has its roots in pre-Achaemenid times when Iran was the neighbour of the civilizations of Old Mesopotamia. In conquering Babylon in 539 B.C., the Achaemenids became the heirs of the last Mesopotamian empire, and for centuries to come one of the capitals of Iran or the capital of the Iranian empire itself was in Mesopotamia.

Looking at the Irano-Islamic city, we must bear in mind that it is an expression of Iran's specific geographic situation, just as it was shaped by a long and checkered history. Thus, in this chapter, before dealing with concrete examples, we have to ask some general questions.

Where are the cities of Iran situated?

How are they supplied with water?

What are the general conditions for the development of urban settlements?

1

What is the relationship between the city and its hinterland?

What are the functions of the city and how did these functions manifest themselves in the appearance of the city in different cultural regions and in different historical periods?

What prototypes of the Irano-Islamic city do we encounter in the cities of Iran between ca. 1000 B.C. and ca. 600 A.D.?

2. THE LAND OF IRAN

2.1. General Features of the Land

Iran is a country of deserts and barren, high mountains. In only a few places does one find contiguous settlements covering wide areas. The country is part of the Eurasian mountain belt, which runs from the Iberian peninsula, through the Alps, the Balkans, the Carpatians, the Taurus and the Pontus, to the Iranian highland rims of the Elburz and Zagros. Iran is also part of the arid belt of the Old World, which stretches from the Sahara in the west across the Arabian peninsula and the Iranian plateau to the deserts of Central Asia in the east. These two belts, which traverse the Old World, intersect in Iran. Thus, mountains and deserts are the two elements that determine the appearance of Iran. Mosaic-like, they intermingle, forming continuously varied combinations.

2.2 Morphology of Settlement Distribution

The bulk of the Iranian population lives in numerous oases of different sizes and in settlements scattered along the foothills of the high mountain chains. A map showing the density of population, which of necessity must be generalized, cannot give a precise idea of the distribution of settlements. But a map that locates all settlements of more than 50,000 inhabitants gives a clearer picture.[2] It also differentiates somewhat the supra-regional centers of Tehran, Mashhad, Tabriz, Isfahan, Abadan, and Shiraz from the regional centers such as Hamadan, Ahvaz, and Rasht, and from subcenters like Zabol, Birjand, or Khoy.

Ill. 1

Ill. 2
A generalized map of the geomorphic regions gives a good impression of the laws that govern settlement distribution. By far the greatest part of the settlements with more than 50,000 inhabitants is located either near the foothills of the Iranian highland rims of the Elburz and Zagros or in intermontane basins.

2

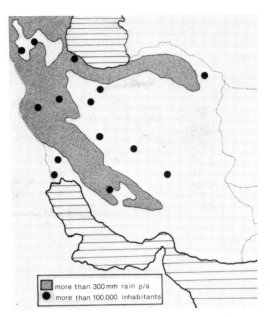

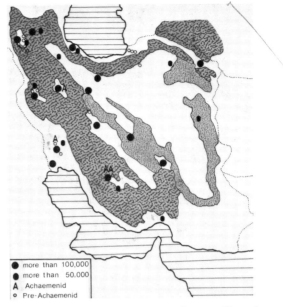

1. Settlements with more than 50,000 inhabitants, major pre-Achaemenid sites, Achaemenid capitals

2. Major Sasanian and medieval cities

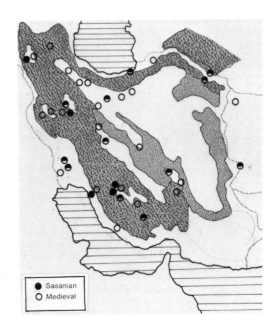

3. Settlements with more than 13,000 inhabitants

2.3. History of Settlement Distribution

The locations of the various settlements are very old. The ancient Achaemenid capitals were near the locations of modern cities: Persepolis and Pasargadae stood near the present Shiraz, Susa near Ahvaz, and Ecbatana at the site of present-day Hamadan. The location of the major pre-Achaemenid sites also fits into this pattern: these sites are concentrated around Rezaiye, Kermanshah, and Ahvaz.

Ill.3   A large number of Sasanian cities can also be found at the site of modern cities or in their vicinity. The same is true for the important medieval Islamic cities, many of which have survived until the present.

2.4. Role of Water

The reason for the location of these large settlements in intermontane basins or along the foothills of the high mountain chains can be explained by the availability of water. The lack of arable space in the tangled relief of the mountainous regions, with more than 300 mm precipitation per annum, the minimum essential for dry-farming, favored the development of larger cities at only a few places, since such cities need a large and easily accessible hinterland, on whose agricultural surplus the city dwellers depend. With the exception of Rasht with more than 100,000 inhabitants in the Caspian lowlands, where there is abundant water, all large cities are located in regions not favored with sufficient annual precipitation. Thus these cities could only come into being and grow where the water supply was assured from sources other than rainfall. Some of them take their water from rivers. The most significant example of this group of cities is Isfahan, which owes its enormous growth potential to the almost inexhaustible water reserves of the Zāyandah-Rūd. Most Iranian cities, such as those cities south of the Elburz and east of the Zagros, depend, however, on ground water, which is brought from the foothills by way of *qanāts*.[3]

3. THE *QANAT*

3.1. Characteristics of the *Qanāt*

The *qanāt* is a subterranean aqueduct. It collects groundwater in the alluvial fans at the foot of high mountains and carries it, following the descent of the terrain, to settlements and fields. The length of the *qanāts* Ill. 4 varies considerably. *Qanāts* 10 kilometers long or longer are quite common. Anyone flying over Iran can see the rings of earth and stones surrounding the *qanāt* shafts. Forming various patterns, the *qanāts*

4

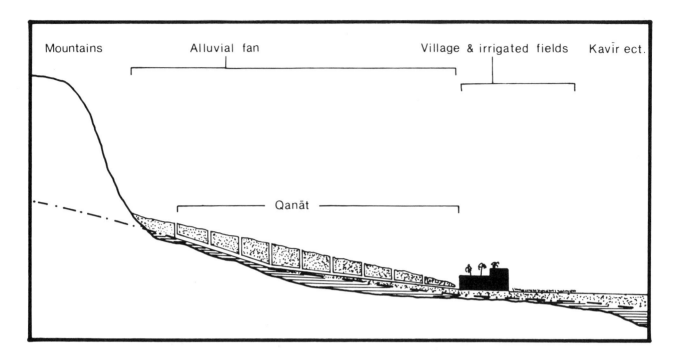

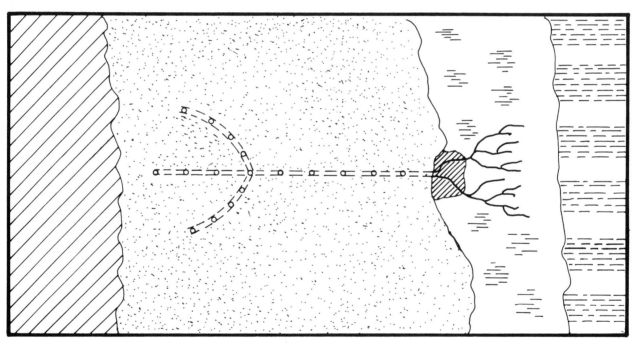

4. Plan and section of a *qanāt*

crisscross the countryside from the mountains to the green patches of the fields and gardens of the settlements.

3.2. Importance of the *Qanāt*

The outstanding importance of the *qanāt* for Iran justifies closer investigation. The art of creating artificial springs by water tunnels originated in the first half of the first millennium B.C. in the Iranian and Armenian highlands. It led to a radical change in the settlement pattern by opening to man new areas hitherto unpopulated. The introduction of the *qanāt* created one of the bases on which the first world empire in history, the Achaemenid state, could be built. The establishment of a network of overland roads, with posts for the army, for communication, administration, and trade, was only possible after the introduction of the *qanāt*. The greatest part of Iranian settlements owe their existence to the *qanāt*, which, due to its complexity and high construction and maintenance costs [4], had a great influence on the social structure and the settlement pattern. Because the construction of a *qanāt* has always been expensive, only the rich can afford them. Of course, the prosperous would dwell near the outlet, the mouth, of the *qanāt*, where the water is fresh and clear, while the poor live farther down, where the water is already warm and contaminated. Furthermore, the owner of the *qanāt* eventually came to be considered the owner of the land it irrigated. Thus *qanāt* irrigation furthered landlordism and promoted its survival until the land reform which was initiated in 1962.

3.3. *Qanāt* Systems of Tehran and Rayy

Ill. 5   Smaller settlements are supplied by one or two *qanāts*, while systems of numerous *qanāts* (carrying water from different directions), converge on larger cities like Tehran. It can easily be seen how the *qanāts* have influenced the orientation of the streets there. Water was distributed in the city through open ditches by means of gravity. A suitable network of alleys and streets had to be laid out close to the *qanāts* in order that the citizens could be provided easily with water. Consequently, the main streets run parallel to the slope, as do the *qanāts*, from which the secondary streets, or alleys, branch off at right angles.

In addition to those *qanāts* that supply the city of Tehran with water, numerous other *qanāts* traverse the fields and gardens south of it. They primarily serve irrigation. Some of them are very old because they belonged to the *qanāt* system of Rayy, the predecessor of Tehran, whose origins go back far into pre-Islamic times.

6

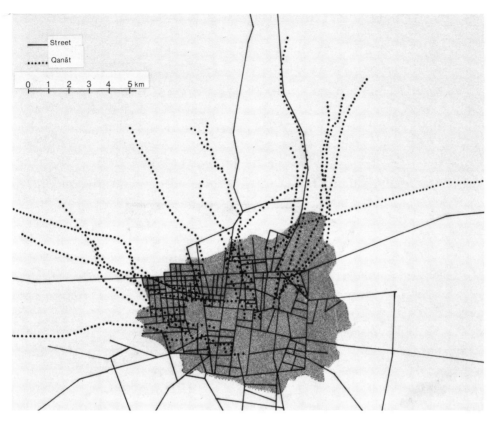

Street

Qanāt

0 1 2 3 4 5 km

5.   The *qanāt* system of Tehran

4. SOCIO-ECONOMIC PRINCIPLES OF URBAN DEVELOPMENT

4.1. Introduction

The morphological and hydrological facts mentioned here have been the primary prerequisites for settlement in Iran. The influence upon settlement of man's development from hunter and gatherer to farmer and herdsman, and later on to craftsman and merchant, is perhaps equally as important. This latter influence is much more fascinating, but it is much debated, and its role in the past still remains obscure. "Socio-archeology"—as I would like to call the branch of archeology devoted to this problem—still has many questions to answer. Nevertheless, some general and of course partly very theoretical answers can be offered. These are answers which can be controlled not only by archeological fieldwork, but by the results of ethnological and cultural-geographical research which

7

help us evaluate and elucidate general theories on the origins of urbanization.

4.2. Definition of the City

The city is a settlement, in most cases circumvallated, with a large population and a high density of both population and buildings.[5] It can only come into existence when the countryside produces food beyond its own requirements. This enables the city dwellers to live without growing their own crops or rearing their own livestock. As a result, they can devote themselves to manufacturing, trade, administration, and other services for the hinterland.[6]

4.3. Division of Labor

The establishment of the city is a direct consequence of the division of labor. We date the roots of this division back into the early neolithic period. At that time, around 8000 B.C., according to our present knowledge, the preconditions for the emergence of the city began to take shape. Within a few millenia the farmer and the herdsman were supplemented by the craftsman, the merchant, the banker, the soldier, and the administrator. Whereas the farmer and the herdsman lived in the countryside, the latter lived in the city.[7] Thus, the city is characterized by the predominance of the secondary sector (that is to say, crafts and industry) and the tertiary sector (that is to say, service), while the primary sector (agriculture) dominates the hinterland.

4.4 The Development of Cities

The genesis of towns or cities can be depicted very easily in a purely mechanistic way: In the course of time, a number of isolated human dwellings grow into small settlements, mostly at places favored by nature, where enough good water can be found, where the wind is not too strong and constant, where the soil is of good quality, and where there is shelter from enemies, among other considerations. At a further stage of development, economic interaction takes place between the individual settlements, raising the most fortunate of them to the level of a borough, or a subcenter, with certain central functions. The prerequisites to becoming a subcenter can be manifold. In addition to the natural factors already mentioned, easy accessibility and convenient distance from the surrounding settlements are obviously important. Finally, the decision of individuals or groups to choose certain places for building palaces or temples also plays a role at this level. These subcenters attract more people who work in the secondary and tertiary sectors. Out of these subcenters, centers (i.e. towns or cities) crystallize which have a complete coverage of the secondary and the tertiary sectors.

4.5. The Relationship of the City to the Hinterland

Many attempts have already been made to depict the relationships that have existed between cities and the surrounding countryside in different historical periods and in different parts of the world. Inquiries dealing with more-or-less remote times have to work with hypotheses, and in them one rarely finds concrete figures. However, geographical studies concerned with present-day conditions provide precise statistical data which elucidate these relationships.[8] Thus, it seems worthwhile to consider a modern example. This presupposes, of course, my own conviction that the mechanisms which have brought about the establishment of present-day cities do not differ in principle from those of earlier times. Modern means of communication and transportation have led only to vaster central place systems.

Malayer, which should serve as an example here, is the center of a district with 130,000 inhabitants and is situated some 250 kilometers southwest of Tehran.[9] The district *(shahristān)* of Malayer comprises 255 villages in which 80 percent of the *shahristān's* population lives. More than half of these villages have less than 500 inhabitants. The majority of the gainfully employed (64 percent) work in agriculture. In the hinterland of Malayer there are 690 shops. Almost all of them are in villages with more than 250 inhabitants. Those places, where there are bazaar-like shops, rose to the position of rural subcenters and so became the centers of the newly founded cooperatives after the land reform of 1962.

The total of 690 shops in the hinterland of Malayer is outnumbered by the 840 shops in Malayer itself which has only 20 percent of the *shahristān's* population. A similar ratio can be found in the secondary sector (that is, in the crafts and industry) if we exclude the more than 1000 carpetmakers in the villages, mostly peasants' wives and children, who are cottage workers and depend almost entirely on the merchants of Malayer.

In addition, the administrative function is concentrated in Malayer, underlining the dominant role of Malayer in its *shahristān*. And Malayer is, I repeat, just one example of many similar central places. Most of the commercial services for the hinterland are provided by Malayer. There the farmers go to sell their produce and to buy industrial products and victuals they do not produce themselves. Malayer is, above all, the center of almost all economic activity in its hinterland and, of course, it profits from it. The city dwellers profit even more from the relationship with the rural population for two additional reasons.

1. The *pīsh-furūsh* system.[10]

2. The organization of the local cottage industry of carpet production, by the bazaar merchants.[11]

The consequence of the notorious lack of cash among the rural population is that many farmers sell their crops in advance *(pīsh-furūsh)* in order to buy the most necessary things in the bazaar of the city. In these transactions the merchants alone gain up to 100 percent profit by the device of manipulating winter and summer prices; they also have a free hand in dictating the prices of the goods the farmer buys. Thus, many farmers enter a vicious circle without a way out and the merchants gain almost complete control of everything that happens in the villages. In fact, they have replaced in many instances the landlords who existed before land reform.

As a consequence of this dependence, farmers have to go to the city to buy even the most common items. An inquiry conducted in southwestern Iran corroborates this. Out of 3000 men:

8 percent go to the city once a month,
53 percent two or three times,
34 percent four to seven times,
5 percent more than eight times.[12]

The organization of carpet manufacture as a cottage industry in the hinterland of Malayer by the merchants of Malayer leads to an additional dependence of the hinterland upon the city. Although a great part of carpet production is performed in the hinterlands, the raw materials are supplied by the merchants and processed on looms owned by them. Thus, the merchant can reduce to a minimum the producers' share in the profit of the carpet industry. (The creation of a cottage industry, however, could lead to the formation of an autonomous center for production, no longer dominated by the city.)

In addition to these two components of the traditional city-hinterland relationship, there was until the sixties a third, which drastically underlines the parasitic role of the city. The city was the place of residence of the landlords, where the profits derived from the hinterland were spent.

Whereas only small landlords lived in Malayer, most of the owners of large holdings (70% of all landlords) lived in Tehran and spend their profits there.[13] In the past, they were forced to live near court or chose to live there to lobby their own interests. In modern times, they were attracted by the higher quality of living that the capital offered.

4.6. The Relationship of the City to the Capital

Just as Malayer lives off its countryside, so Tehran, the capital of Iran, lives off Malayer and all the other cities of Iran. Forty-four percent of all the goods sold in Malayer come from wholesale markets in Tehran, while all other cities account for an aggregate of only twenty six percent.[14] Thus, the wholesale trade in Malayer is dominated by the markets and merchants of Tehran. Nor is Malayer an isolated instance: More than 75 percent of all wholesale trade profits in Iran accrue to Tehran.

5. APPEARANCE OF THE CITY

5.1. The Realization of the Appearance of the City from its Function

As its most apparent feature, the city has been walled in almost all civilizations and periods of history. This was considered necessary in order to protect the houses and businesses within the city, as well as its riches. The city not only provides protection, but, as I have indicated, the city is the seat of government, the center of the intellectual and religious life, the locus of economic activity, and the dwelling place of the population engaged in these functions.[15]

We find these four fundamental functions of the city in all historical periods and in all civilizations. They thus can be considered as the significant features defining the general notion of "city." A division of these fundamental functions into sub-functions leads to a certain differentiation between the medieval and the pre-medieval cities of Europe and the Near East on the one hand, and cities of some other civilizations on the other. But it ultimately shows how similar the cities in all historical periods and in all civilizations are.[16] We do encounter differences and peculiarities between individual cities, if we ask ourselves how these urban functions take concrete form in the appearance of the city, i.e., how in distinct periods and distinct civilizations man as builder and schemer responded to these general functional demands and how he gave them a physical form.

Here, we are not going to discuss the cities of pre-Columbian America or the Far East. But let us rather direct our attention to the Islamic city, which is our main concern here, as well as to the ancient oriental city and the Greco-Roman city.

5.2. The Appearance of the City in Ancient Mesopotamia

First, let us look at the ancient oriental city, more precisely that of ancient Mesopotamia, where "we are confronted with a remarkable variety of civilizations, each of which created a distinctive assemblage of urban features..., which were blurred, and reduced by repeated invasions..., internal social and economic changes."[17] Although neither philologists nor archeologists have been able to illuminate fully the reasons for this variety, observations of a more general kind may be offered. They will help us to understand how the Iranian city, for all its peculiarities, shares some of the characteristics of the older oriental cities of Mesopotamia.

In ancient Mesopotamia the palace and temple represent the first two of the four basic functions of the city, those of the seat of government and the intellectual and religious center. The third function, the place of non-agrarian economic activities, is carried out in the market and the craft workshops. The spatial relation between these individual components of the city changes at different historical periods and in different parts of ancient Mesopotamia. The palace, the temple, the workshops (very often closely connected with the latter), and the living quarters of higher-ranking citizens were inside the city walls, while the market was now located within and now outside the city's walls.[18]

This scheme of organization seems to have been valid for a considerable number of cities in southern Mesopotamia, so long as they did not
Ill. 6   exceed a certain size, that is if they conformed to the type of an "ideal" city as it appears to be represented on a relief from Ninive. Here, the city is surrounded by an almost circular wall with towers. The palace is in the center. The other two buildings, similarly depicted, are most likely temples. A large section of the relief depicts craftsmen in their workshops.

As soon as cities passed a certain "critical" number of inhabitants, as, for example, Ur at the end of the second millennium B.C., a function-oriented differentiation of the individual urban components took place.
Ill. 7   Here, in Ur, living quarters, crafts, religious and intellectual activities, and trade (retail and wholesale) are closely associated.[19] The layout of Ur bears a striking resemblance to peripheral sections of traditional Islamic
Ill. 8   cities, such as the Dar-Dasht quarter of Isfahan. Religious buildings, schools, hostels for foreign merchants, and shops are all located on one of

the main axes of intra-urban communication, while the workshops of the crafts lie somewhat apart. There is one important difference, however. In Ur, there is no bazaar. In Isfahan, shops line the axis forming a continuous bazaar; in Ur the shops are dispersed in small groups.

A comparison between peripheral quarters of Ur and another peripheral quarter of Isfahan discloses further similarity: In both we find dead-end lanes and houses with internal courtyards, which are two of the most distinctive characteristics of the oriental city. In Ur as in Isfahan dead-end lanes branch off from the primary and secondary axes of intraurban communication. They lead to groups of houses, the rooms of which are built around internal courtyards.

Ill. 9 and 10

6. Assyrian relief showing a Mesopotamian city

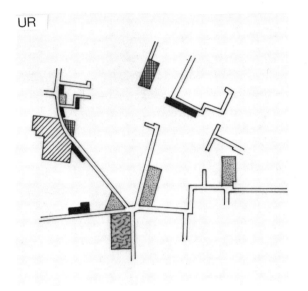

7. A quarter of Ur

8. A quarter of Isfahan

9. A quarter of Ur

10. A quarter of Isfahan

14

In the ancient Mesopotamian city shops, workshops, hostels, and religious and cultural edifices were located according to a strict, invariable scheme. This observation can be extended somewhat further. We not only encounter variability of location in connection with purely economic and secondary religious and cultural buildings; it can also be observed in the case of the central institutions of the ancient Mesopotamian city, the palace and the temple. Their location does not conform to a strict canon but changes at different times and in different regions. In southern Mesopotamia the palace and temple were generally separated from each other, but they could have been situated anywhere within the circumvallation. Later, in Assyria, they were built together and located either in the center of the city or abutting the inner side of the city walls.

This palace-temple complex, the expression of the amalgamation of the functions of the priest and the ruler, finds its material expression in the architectural form of the citadel.[20] The citadel was built within the circumvallation, but it was separated from the rest of the city by walls as strong as the city's own exterior walls. As the seat of government, the citadel left its imprint on the oriental city for centuries to come, and the citadel-city of ancient Mesopotamia is one of the formal prototypes of the Islamic oriental city, be it Maghrebian, Syrian, or Iranian.

5.3. The Appearance of an Ancient Greek City

In the region shaped by the Greek genius, the development of the city took a different direction.[21] Aristotle, for example, thought the citadel a structure appropriate to oligarchies and monarchies but as absolutely inappropriate for the Greek concept of the state.[22] Thus, indeed, we encounter settlements that were laid out like citadels, such as Mycene or Tiryns in the time of Homeric heroes, but observe an entirely different type of settlement in the time of the Greek democracies. This latter type of settlement has its roots in the democratic constitution of the Greek village.

The Greek city of the sixth and fifth centuries B.C. had a much more organic relationship with its hinterland than the oriental city. It was not a parasite on the hinterland. Good proof of this is the fact that many Greek cities did not allow their citizens to become merchants. That is, the early Greek city was a kind of linear enlargement of the village, whose democratic inner structure was preserved. The town hall, agora, gymnasium, public fountain, theater, and temple, the prerequisites of a city, as Pausanias wrote, were not manifestations of the city's distinct social structure, but expressions of a refined style of life which took its standards from the village.[23]

15

This Greek city of the sixth and fifth centuries B.C. is different from the type of city we call Hellenistic or Greco-Roman, the plan of which bears the name "Hippodamean" after the architect Hippodamus of Miletus (who died before 410 B.C.). In some of its physical aspects, that is, the irregularity of its plan and its twisted, unpaved lanes without a sewage system, the ancient Greek city was closer to some ancient oriental city than to its Hippodamean successor. In the latter, the basic element of spatial organization was a chessboard-like system of paved streets. Into this system all buildings of the secondary and tertiary sectors were integrated, as, for example, in Miletus, the town of Hippodamus. The city is built on a peninsula, whose contours were disregarded in the planning. The important public buildings lie on a strip in the middle of the city.

Alexander the Great spread the Hippodamean pattern of city planning far to the east as he founded cities on his way to India and back. In Italy, too, Greek colonists built cities according to the Hippodamean plan. There, however, they were synthesized with the ancient Italic principle of the two axes, the *cardo* and the *decumanus,* which intersected in the center of the city.[24] These western concepts of city planning influenced builders in the east to lay out either a purely Hippodamean city or an Italo-Hippodamean city. Between the fourth century B.C. and the fourth century A.D., wherever Hellenistic kings or Roman emperors ruled, cities were built following these two western schemes.

Many of these cities were conquered by the Arabs in the seventh century A.D. Thus, the Hippodamean or Italo-Hippodamean city joined the ancient oriental city as a second formative influence on the plan of the Islamic city. Even today many Islamic cities show traces of their original Hippodamean plan. In Damascus, for example, we can easily detect the contours of the Hippodamean streets and lanes, which the present-day streets and lanes partly follow.

5.4. The Appearance of the Islamic City

The Islamic city became the heir of the two different types of cities: the oriental despotic city and the Hellenistic-Roman democratic city. The Arab language, the new religion of Islam, a quickly developing trade between the east and the west of the Islamic world, and an extraordinary mobility of population united vast parts of the Old World, parts that for centuries had been divided into a Roman-Byzantine and Iranian hemisphere. In this area of Islamic civilization cities developed common features regardless of when they were founded and regardless of the original plans in which they were laid out. Thus, presupposing a

16

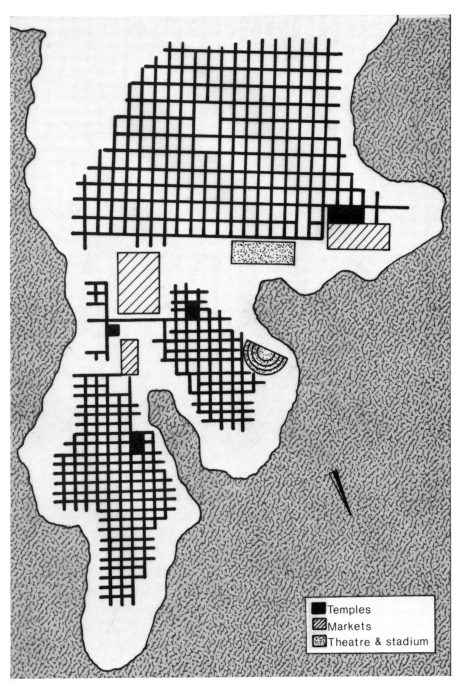

Temples
Markets
Theatre & stadium

11. Plan of Miletus

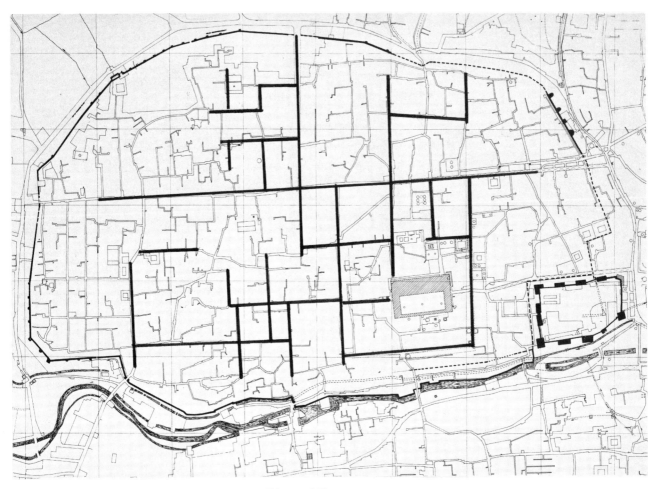

12. Plan of Damascus

homogeneous civilization on the one hand and a regional individuality
on the other, we can speak without any hesitation of *the* Islamic city,
which was more influenced by its oriental than by its Greco-Roman
heritage.

Let us try to form a general idea of the Islamic city and look for its
physiognomic peculiarities and the rules which influenced its physical
appearance. Here it seems opportune to recall the four basic functions
which are the significant features defining the notion of "city" in general.
A city serves as

1. the seat of government;

2. the center of intellectual and religious life;

18

3. the place of non-agrarian economic activities; and

4. the dwelling place of a population which is not employed in the primary sector.

In the Islamic city these four functions are embodied in specific Islamic institutions as well as in institutions we may find in cities of other civilizations. The seat of government is located in the citadel (3) with barracks, and the palace. The latter may sometimes be outside the citadel too. Religious and intellectual life is embodied in the mosques and *madrasas* (schools), in shrines, and other places of worship and learning. The nonagrarian economic activities take place in shops, warehouses, workshops, and the hostels (caravansarais, *khāns*) for the foreign merchants. All are unified and spatially coordinated in the bazaar. The nonagrarian population inhabits living quarters situated within or outside the city's walls.

The city walls (1), which, with a few exceptions, have a polygonal plan, contain a variable number of gates (2). Through some of these gates, overland roads (4) enter the city. The most frequented of these overland roads run through *extra muros* suburbs (5), where economic subcenters very often have been developed, generally near the gates. Within the city's walls, the overland roads continue as the main axes of intra-urban communication (6). The Great Mosque (7) is located on the main axis, or very near to it, and in many cases close to the center of the city. Near the mosque there are often administrative institutions (8), and at least one of the important *madrasas* (9).

Ill. 13A

Ill. 13B

Ill. 13C

The endless flow of people through the main routes of intra-urban communications attracts the trade and the crafts, that is, the larger the numbers of people that pass by, the more potential customers there are. Thus the major cross streets are lined with chains of shops and workshops forming the bazaar. To protect customers and shopkeepers against the sun and rain the bazaar sections of the axes are covered either with wooden roofs or vaults. The center of the bazaar is at the place of the highest density of intraurban circulation, i.e., near the crossing of two or more axes. There, the most precious goods are sold. Shops with less expensive goods and the workshops of the crafts can be found at some distance from the center in the direction of the gates. Concentrated near the gates are shops of merchants and craftsmen who deal in goods bought by the rural population.

Ill. 13D

The bazaar [25] is the most distinctive characteristic of the Islamic city. It is the control-center of the city's economy as well as that of the

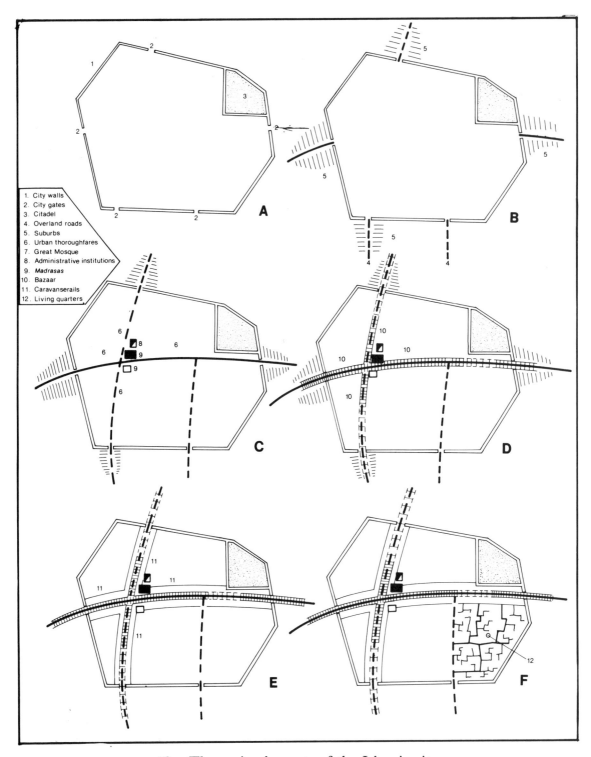

1. City walls
2. City gates
3. Citadel
4. Overland roads
5. Suburbs
6. Urban thoroughfares
7. Great Mosque
8. Administrative institutions
9. *Madrasas*
10. Bazaar
11. Caravanserails
12. Living quarters

13. The main elements of the Islamic city

hinterland. There was nothing like the bazaar in pre-Islamic times or in other civilizations. Here, wholesale and retail trade, the crafts and industry, as well as banking are concentrated. All of this is arranged as a spatial contiguity and an organizational whole. The bazaar can develop linearly, that is, along the intraurban main-axes, or it can spread over the center of the city. In most cases we find a combination of both types.

Behind the shops and workshops of the bazaar there are the caravansarais, the establishments of the long-distance and wholesale trade, the courtyards for the crafts and industry, warehouses, and of-fices (11).

Ill. 13E

The bazaar has no residential function at all. The living quarters are separated from it and are scattered over the whole city (12). Access between the individual houses and the rest of the city is provided by secondary roads and by dead-end lanes, which branch off from them. These dead-end lanes can be very short, but they also may form very complicated systems, as for example in Aleppo where one principal road gives access to no less than eighty-two houses. Some small mosques, a few of the *madrasas, hammāms* and small bazaars with a few shops which supply the residents with goods for every day use and common food staff, may be found in the residential quarters.

Ill. 13F

Ill. 14

Ill. 15

6. PRE-ISLAMIC IRANIAN CITIES

6.1. Introduction

Now, we must at last return to Iran, and we shall initially try to form some notion of what the pre-Islamic Iranian cities looked like. The task is not a simple one. In the Near East, including Iran, archeological fieldwork may reveal in the future characteristics we cannot think of today. Our present knowledge of older Iranian urbanism consists of separate bits and pieces which at best provide a kind of patchwork overview.

6.2. Old Iranian/Achaemenid Cities

At the beginning of the first millennium B.C., Medes and Persians emigrated from the north into present-day Iran. From this period on we can speak of Iranian cities. The earliest representations of these cities are only shown schematically on Assyrian reliefs. However, by drawing upon Herodotus' description of Agbatana, the Hamadan of today, which was the capital of the Median state, we can get an idea of the essential elements of the Median city. Herodotus writes: ". . . the Medes . . . dwell in scattered villages. . . ." King Deioces (who is most probably the

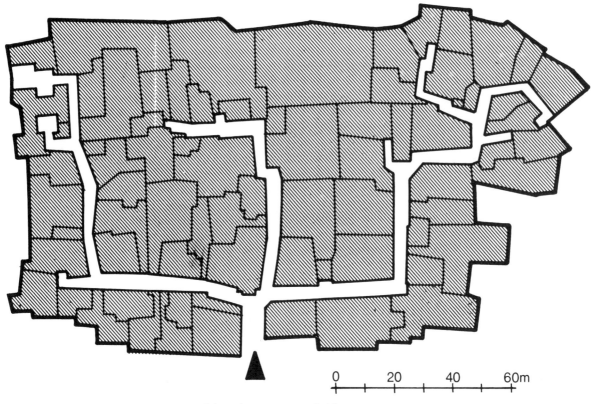

0   20   40   60m

14. A quarter of Aleppo

Kyaxares, 625-584 B.C., of other sources) "required them to build a single great city now called Agbatana, the walls of which are of great size and strength, rising in circles one within the other. The plan of the place is that each wall should out-top one beyond it by the battlements. The nature of the ground, which is a gentle hill, favors this arrangement in some degree, but it was mainly effected by art. The number of the circles is seven, the royal palace and the treasuries standing within the last." [26]

Ill. 16   Herodotus describes Agbatana as a round city, surrounded by several rings of walls which rise one above the other. An Assyrian relief from the eighth century B.C. where the Median city of Kishesim is depicted, conforms to the urban principles described by Herodotus. Here we see a sequence of walls rising one above the other and may assume the highest wall to be the wall of the palace. This location of the palace at the highest point of the settlement seems to have been one of the characteristics of early Iranian cities. Already at Siyalk (about 1000 B.C.) there is evidence of a terrace on which the residence of the ruler is thought to have been located.[27] Terraces also rise above Achaemenid settlements.

22

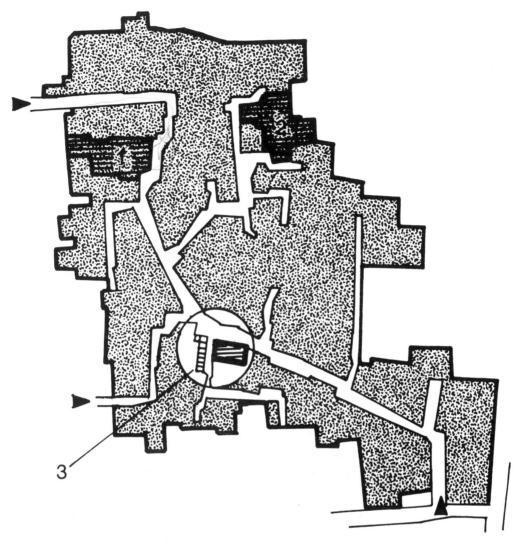

3

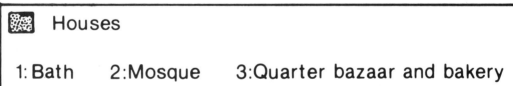

Houses

1: Bath   2: Mosque   3: Quarter bazaar and bakery

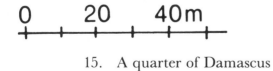

0   20   40m

15.   A quarter of Damascus

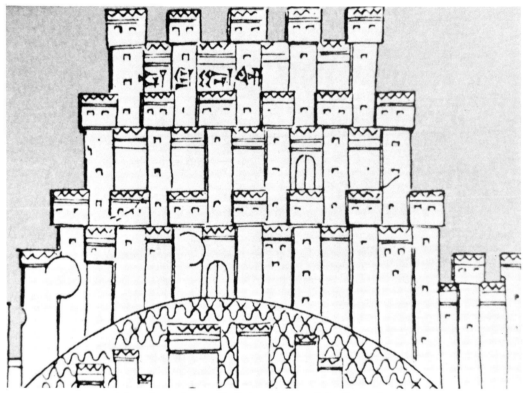

16.   Assyrian relief showing a Median city

The earliest examples were found in Khuzistan (Masjid-i Sulaimān and Bard-i Nishāndih).

Ill. 17   The oldest inner-Iranian terrace can be seen in Pasargadae. Most probably it was built by King Cambyses I (600-588 B.C.). This terrace is essentially the same as that built in Persepolis. There, the palace, the treasure house, and other royal buildings stand on the terrace that rises above the plan of Persepolis.

Both Pasargadae and Persepolis were surrounded by low, thin walls, polygonal in plan, which differ from those of the Median cities, with their elaborate fortifications.[28] This is not at all surprising since Persepolis and Pasargadae were not the capitals of a state threatened by mighty enemies, but the capitals of the most powerful empire under the sun.

6.3. Alexandrian and Seleucid Cities

Alexander the Great's victory over the Achaemenids diffused Greek ideas as far east as India. The numerous cities he founded in Iran and India followed the Hippodamean plan. Thus, the Hippodamean scheme became known in the east.

24

Alexander and his successors, the Seleucids, were followed by the Iranian Parthians, who preferred to build round cities. Examples of the latter can be found in both the eastern and western extensions of the Parthian Empire.

The nucleus of the city of Merv (today in the Soviet Union) was founded by Alexander the Great. It was destroyed in 293 B.C. and rebuilt as a Hippodamean city by Antiochos I (280-261), who named it Antiochaia Margiana. This Hippodamean nucleus was surrounded, in the Parthian period, by a settlement which had a wall roughly round in shape.[29] The most impressive example of a round Parthian city, however, can be found in the west, in northwestern Iraq. Hatra is surrounded by two round walls.[30] In the center of the city there is a wide temple complex. In this, Hatra resembles another Parthian city, Dārāb, in southern Iran.[31] Here, the perfectly circular mud wall encircles two large rock formations. On one of these are the ruins of a castle. Most likely there was a temple on the other.

6.5. Sasanian Cities

The round city of Fīrūz-Abād/Gūr is situated near Dārāb. This unexcavated place with a temple in its center is the site of the first Sasanian capital, Ardashīr-Khurra.[32] The city was founded by Ardashīr I (226-240 A.D.), the first Sasanian king.

Ill. 18

17.   The terrace of Pasargadae

18.   Aerial view of Fīrūz-Abād

Ardashīr's son, Shāpūr I (240-271 A.D.), built his capital Bīshāpūr
northwest of Fīrūz-Abād. After his spectacular victory over the Romans
in the battle of Edessa in 260 A.D., in which emperor Valerian became his
prisoner, many Roman prisoners of war were brought to Iran. They were
employed in the building of Bīshāpūr. They left their imprint, as the
Ill. 19 Hippodamean plan of Bīshāpūr indicates.[33] They also exerted a strong
influence on the decorative art of the city, as is shown by the mosaics
found there.[34] The use of the Hippodamean plan was not restricted to
Bīshāpūr in Shāpūr's times. Nīshāpūr in northeastern Iran and Fun-
dīshāpūr in Khuzistan were also built as Hippodamean cities. And more,
the Hippodamean plan can be considered the favored plan of the cities
founded by the Sasanians.

26

19.   Aerial view of Bīshāpūr

6.6. Conclusion

In summary, in pre-Islamic Iran different plans were used to lay out cities. This should not surprise us if we consider the political role the Achaemenids and Sasanians played in Near Eastern history. They were not only the heirs of the ancient oriental empires but also of Alexander the Great. Thus the Iranian city must reflect all these different civilizations, as precisely it does.

1. The polygonal contours of Persepolis and Pasargadae, generally the distinctive characteristic of cities which have undergone gradual growth, we find in many ancient oriental cities, post-Achaemenid cities, and medieval and post-medieval cities.

2. The Hippodamean city plan of Alexandrian and Seleucid times was used by the Sasanians. The "grid" pattern of streets can already be found in Urartu (from the ninth to the seventh centuries B.C.) [35] Most probably some Assyrian cities were laid out in this manner too. [36] In the Islamic period there is evidence that newly opened areas of old cities were planned following a "grid" pattern.[37]

3. Finally, the round city, like the Hippodamean city, is the product of

planning. There is evidence that round cities existed in pre-Parthian times. Zinjirli in northern Syria, which was founded at the end of the second millennium B.C., had two circular walls.[38] The palace and the temple were in the center of this city. Hatra, Dārāb, and Fīrūz-Abād were constructed this way. In the early 'Abbāsid period the round city of al-Manṣūr was built at the site of present-day Baghdad.[39] Manṣūr's grandson, Hārūn al-Rashīd, built a similar but smaller palace-camp near Raqqa in Syria.[40] And later settlements with circular walls can be found as well in Iran and Afghanistan.

NOTES

1. Except in familiar geographic names the transcription system used here is that of the *International Journal of Middle East Studies*.

2. G. Schweizer, "Bevölkerungsentwicklung and Verstädterung in Iran," *Geographische Rundschau*, 23 (1971), 347.

3. C. Braun, *Tehran, Marrakesch und Madrid. Ihre Wasserversorgung mit Hilfe von Qanaten. Eine stadtgeographische Konvergenz auf kulturhistorischer Grundlage* (Bonner Geographische Abhandlungen, Heft 52) (Bonn, 1974); P. English: "The Origin and Spread of Qanats in the Old World," *Proc. Americ. Phil. Soc.*, 112, 3; C. Troll, "Qanatbewässerung in der Altern und Neuen Welt," *Mitt. d. Osterr. Geogr. Ges.* 1963. Heft 3; E. Wulff, *The Traditional Crafts of Persia* (Cambridge, Mass., 1966), 249-254.

4. The construction of the *qanāt* demands great technical skill and geological knowledge and presupposes an exact survey of the terrain. This has led to the development of the respected craft of the *muqannī*, the *qanāt* builder. What requirements a *muqannī* must meet and what techniques and knowledge he has to master are set down in a book written 1000 or so years ago, the *Inbāt al-miyāh al-khafiyya* or *The Disclosure of Hidden Waters*. Its author was a *muqannī* from Karaj near Tehran. The book describes the means to determine the position of a *qanāt*, to survey the terrain, to dig the *qanāt*, and to master unexpected problems while digging. Al-Karajī, Muhammad, *Kitāb inbāt al-miyāh al-khafiyya*. (Persian translation: *Istikhrāj-i ābhā-yi pinhanī* (Tehran 1344/1966). 1344/1966).

5. Some of the many books dealing with the city in general are: E. Jones, *Towns and Cities* (Oxford, 1970); L. Mumford, *The City in History* (Baltimore, Md., 1966); M. Weber, *The City* (Engl. translation) (Glencoe, Ill. 1958.)

6. Cf. A. H. Hourani, "The Islamic City in the Light of Recent Research," A. H. Hourani and S. M. Stern (ed.), *The Islamic City* (Oxford, 1970), 9.

7. How controversial the question of the origin of cities still is may be seen in: G. Childe, *What Happened in History* (Baltimore, Md., 1964); G. Daniel, *The First Civilizations. The Archaeology of Their Origins* (London, 1968); J. Jacobs, *Economy of Cities* (New York, 1969); R. Mc. C. Adams, "The Study

of Ancient Mesopotamian Settlement Patterns and the Problem of Urban Origins," *Sumer*, 25 (1969), 111-124.

8. Cf. H. Bobek, "Uber einige funktionelle Stadttypen und ihre Beziehung zum Lande," *C. R. Congr. Internat. Géogr. Amsterdam 1938*, vol. 2, Sect. 3a (Leiden, 1938), 88-102; E. Wirth, "Die Beziehung der orientalisch-islamischen Stadt zum umgebenden Land. Ein Beitrag zur Theorie des Rentenkapitalismus," E. Meynen (ed.); *Geographie heute. Einheit und Vielfalt. Ernst Pleve zum 65. Geburtstag* (Wiesbaden, 1973), 323-333.

9. M. Momeni, *Malayer und sein Umland. Entwicklung, Struktur und Funktion einer Kleinstadt in Iran* (Marburger Geographische Schriften, Heft 68) (Marburg/Lahn, 1976); another excellent study of the city-hinterland relationship in Iran is: M. E. Bonine, *Yazd and its Hinterland. A Central Place System of Dominance in the Central Iranian Plateau* (Austin, Texas, 1975).

10. E. Ehlers, *Traditionelle und moderne Formen der Landwirtschaft in Iran. Siedlung, Wirtschaft und Agrarsozialstruktur im nördlichen Khuzistan seit dem Ende des 19. Jahrhunderts* (Marburger Geographische Schriften, Heft 64) (Marburg, 1975), 136-142; E. Ehlers, "Dezful und sein Umland. Einige Anmerkungen zu den Umlandbeziehungen iranischer Klein- und Mittelstädte," G. Schweizer (ed.), *Beiträge zur Geographie orientalischer Städte und Märkte* (Beihefte zum Tübinger Atlas des Vorderen Orients, Reihe B, Nr. 24) (Wiesbaden, 1977), 147-171; H.K.S. Lodi, "Preharvest Sales of Agricultural Produce in Iran," *Monthly Bulletin of Agric. Economics and Statistics*, 14, no. 6 (1965), 1-4; M. Momeni, *op. cit.*, 181 f.

11. M. Momeni, *op. cit.*, 182; for another region cf. M. Bazin, "Le travail du tapis dans la région de Qom (Iran Central)," *Bull. Soc. Languedoc Géogr.*, 7 (1973), 83-92; the far-reaching connections between the carpet cottage industry and the markets are depicted by E. Wirth, *Der Orientteppich und Europa* (Erlanger Geographische Arbeiten, Heft 37) (Erlangen, 1976), 71-95.

12. F.G.L. Gremliza, *Ecology of Endemic Diseases in the Dez Irrigation Pilot Area. A Report to the Khuzistan Water and Power Authority and Plan Organisation* (New York, 1962), 90.

13. M. Momeni, *op. cit.*, 170.

14. M. Momeni, *op. cit.*, 113-117.

15. The first who attempted a broad analysis of the city's functions was M. Weber, *The City* (Engl. translation) (Glencoe, Ill., 1958); the function of the oriental city in particular is dealt with by E. Wirth, "Die orientalische Stadt. Ein Uberblick aufgrund jüngster Forschungen zur materiellen Kultur," *Saeculum*, 26 (1975), 45-94.

16. E. Wirth, *op. cit.*, 51-53.

17. A.L. Oppenheim, *Ancient Mesopotamia. Portrait of a Dead Civilization* (Chicago 1964), 127.

18. W. Röllig, "Der altmesopotamische Markt," *Die Welt des Orients*, 8 (1976), 288-295.

19. C. L. Wooley, "Excavations at Ur, 1930-31," *The Antiquaries Journal*, 11 (1931), 343-381.

20. A. L. Oppenheim, *op. cit.*, 130.

21. Cf. A. Kriesis, *Greek Town Building* (Athens, 1965); R. Martin and J. Picard, *L'Urbanisme dans la Grèce antique* (Paris, 1956); R. E. Wycherley, *How the Greeks Built Cities*, 2nd. ed. (London, 1962).

22. *Politics*, IV, 9.

23. *Description of Greece*, X, 4.

24. Cf. P. Grimal, *Les villes romaines* (Paris, 1954); F. Haverfield, *Ancient Town Planning* (London, 1913).

25. Cf. E. Wirth, "Zum Problem des Ba-

zars *(sūq, çarşi)*. Versuch einer Begriffsbestimmung und Theorie des traditionellen Wirtschaftszentrums der orientalisch-islamischen Stadt," *Der Islam,* 51 (1974), 203-260 and 52 (1975), 6-46.

26. *History,* I, 96-98.
27. R. Ghirshman, *Fouilles de Sialk, près de Kashan, 1933, 1934, 1937* (Paris 1938-1939).
28. E. F. Schmidt, *Flights over Ancient Cities of Iran* (Chicago 1940), pl. 2 and 15.
29. G. A. Pugatschenkowa, *Puti raswitija architektury juschnogo Turkmenistana pory rabowladenija i feodalisma* (Moscow, 1958), 42.
30. F. Safar, *al- Hadr madīnat ash-shams* (Baghdād, 1974), 10.
31. A. Stein, "An archaeological tour in Gedrosia," *Memoirs of the Archaeological Survey of India,* 43 (1931), pl. 10.
32. A. Stein, "An archaeological tour in the ancient Persis," *Iraq,* 3 (1936), 112-125, 118-122.
33. R. Ghirshman, *Bîchâpour* (Fouilles de Châpour I) (Paris, 1971), 27
34. R. Ghirshman, *Bîchâpour. Les mosaiques Sassanides* (Fouilles de Châpour II) (Paris, 1956).
35. C. A. Burney, "Urartian fortresses and towns in the Van region," *Anatolian Studies,* 7 (1957), 37-53.
36. A. L. Oppenheim, *op. cit.,* 138.
37. See below, Ill. 45.
38. H. V. Luschan: *Ausgrabungen in Sendschirli,* II (Berlin, 1898), pl. 29.
39. J. Lassner: *The Topography of Baghdad in the Early Middle Ages* (Detroit, 1970).
40. F. Sarre and E. Herzfeld, *Archäologische Reise im Euphrat und Tigris-Gebiet* (Forschungen zur islamischen Kunst, I) (Berlin, 1911), I, 161 f. and III, pl. 25.

CHAPTER TWO

Herat—An
Indo-Iranian City?

1. LOCATION AND HISTORY OF HERAT

Herat is the westernmost large city of Afghanistan.[1] It is situated in a
fertile river oasis and surrounded by a multitude of villages. Due to its
geographical position, the city was the gateway to India. Alexander the
Great had passed through it, as had the trade between India and the
Near East up to very recent times.

Herat is also a gateway to the north. Between Istanbul and the
Himalayas there is no place where the northern mountain rims of the
central Near Eastern basins are so low and easy to pass as they are north
of Herat. This fortunate location naturally made Herat into a place of
eminent strategical importance. For this reason, Herat was often
conquered. Several times it was destroyed, but the inhabitants always
managed to recover within a short period. Although its history is a
succession of ups and downs, Herat never had to share the fate of many
other Iranian cities, that is, to suffer, on the one hand, a partial
depopulation or, on the other, to be razed to the ground never to be
inhabited again.

2. MODERN HERAT

In the second half of the nineteenth century and at the beginning of the twentieth Europeans came to Herat, and the British wrote extensively about the area.[2] One British officer wrote:

> Herat is a dirty town. The small lanes, crooked and narrow which branch from the main thoroughfares, are roofed and their gloom offers safe harbourage for the perpetration of every possible offence. The breadth of the streets is only 12 feet, but in their narrowest parts even this space is reduced. Pools of stagnant water left by the rains, piles of refuse thrown from the houses, together with dead cats, dogs and the excrements of human beings, mingle their effluvia in these low tunnels.[3]

Ill. 20

This statement is still valid as far as the old city is concerned. It does not apply to the eastern sections of Herat which were built in this century, the Shahr-i Nau, or "New City." In this part of the city one can find tree-lined boulevards which pass by parks and large gardens. Some are planned to form vistas, which are copied from the nineteenth- and twentieth-century European planners. Smaller streets branch off in a regular pattern from the boulevards, and they are lined by houses built in European style and by villas in well-kept gardens full of trees. In this part of the city we find modern hotels, whose guests are mostly tourists visiting the ruins around Herat. Nor would the western and the northwestern parts of the new city—which represent the first periods of modern building activities—have inspired our traveller to make the statement quoted above. Although the building density is here considerably higher than in the eastern part of the city, it became the eldorado for generations of young people who wished to escape for brief spells of time from Western civilization to be enchanted by the exotic atmosphere of Herat.

3. NINETEENTH-CENTURY HERAT

As there are good and reliable descriptions of Herat in the nineteenth century and the beginning of the twentieth, we can easily form an idea of what the city looked like about a hundred years ago. There are even some

Ill. 24

old maps, the most informative of which is the one drawn by a German officer, Oskar von Niedermayer, who led a small military expedition to Afghanistan in 1916 and 1917.[4]

32

20. Map of Herat

From Niedermayer's map, we can see that the city was nearly square in plan, measuring 1500 meters from east to west and by 1600 meters from north to south and was oriented to the cardinal points of the compass. It was surrounded by a wall, which in its lowest portions measured 7 meters in height and which stood on a mound of about 14 meters in height. In front of the mound a wide and deep ditch ran around the city.[5] Only a few remains of the walls are extant, but pictures taken some sixty years ago show the strength of Herat's fortifications.

Ill. 21 and 22

There were five gates in the wall: the Qandahār gate in the middle of the south side, the Khushk gate in the middle of the east side, the Iraq gate in the middle of the west side, the Qīchāq gate in the middle of the eastern section of the north side, and the Malik gate in the middle of the western section of this same side.

Ill. 23

21.   The southwest corner of the wall of Herat in 1916

22.   The north wall of Herat in 1916

3.2 The Bazaar

Four streets led from the Qandahār, the Khushk, the Iraq, and the
Malik gates and met in the center of the city. They were 12 to 15 feet
wide, though they have been broadened so that traffic can pass. These
four streets were (and still are) the location of the bazaar of Herat. They
were lined with shops and workshops, not much different from those of
today. The four sections of the bazaar met at a domed structure, the
chahār-sū, the "four directions." They were roofed over to within a short
distance from the *chahār-sū* with masonry, further on with wooden rafters
and thatch. The *chahār-su* has become a victim of modern widening of
streets. On the map of Niedermayer as well as on a map drawn in 1842[6],   Ill. 24
this *chahār-sū* is not depicted as a simple crossroad. Around a circular
central space is a square, formed by lanes, which is connected with both

35

23. The Iraq gate of Herat after Hamilton

the center and the four bazaar streets. Most likely this representation refers to a structure similar to the Chahār-sū Chītsāzhā, the cloth imprinters *chahār-sū,* in Isfahan.

Ill. 25

There is a similar structure, the Ṭāq-i Zargarān, in Bukhara. This structure has exactly the same location as the *chahār-sū* of Herat. It stretches over the intersection of the two old axes of intraurban communication. The buildings in Isfahan and Bukhara consist of octagonal central spaces covered by huge domes which are surrounded by passages covered by small domes. In the corners of the central spaces there are four shops, and the passages are lined by shops on both sides.

The Chahār-sū Chītsāzhā in Isfahan, which was built in the time of Shāh ʿAbbās I, and the *ṭāq* in Bukhara are roughly contemporary. We know that at the end of the sixteenth and the beginning of the seventeenth centuries craftsmen emigrated from Herat to Bukhara and Isfahan. We also know a *chahār-sū* existed in Herat as early as the fif-

24.   Niedermayer's map of the inner city of Herat

37

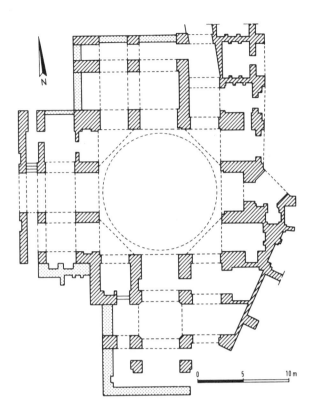

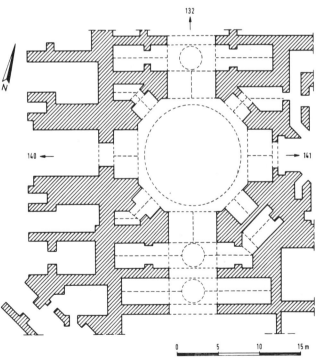

25. The Chahār-sū Chītsazhā in Isfahan and the Ṭāq-i Zargarān in Bukhara

teenth century.[7] Thus, it is possible that the *chahār-sū* of Herat served as a prototype of the structures in Isfahan and Bukhara and looked like these do now.

Caravansarais were situated near the *chahār-sū* and south of it. (Some of the buildings from the nineteenth century are still preserved.) Foreign Ill. 26 merchants lived in these during their stay in Herat. The buildings included shops and storage areas on the ground floor and, above, bedrooms. In addition to the caravansarais built in the traditional style, in the first decades of this century, large two-storied buildings were Ill. 27 constructed. They serve today as offices of wholesale firms and very often also house small factories, in particular textile industries. Caravansarai-like buildings, that is, one or two-storied structures with isolated rooms built around a courtyard, are still being built. Most of them have shops on the ground floor while the upper floors serve as cheap hotels.

To provide drinking water for the bazaar and the adjacent sections of the city there were, in several places of the city, huge reservoirs covered by high domes. Most of them are still used; others are empty, as is the biggest reservoir of the city, which was built in the period of Shāh Ill. 28 'Abbās I.

In the north, the north-south axis led to the gate of the citadel and then followed the ditch of the citadel westward until it reached the Malik gate. This portion of the old main axis of the city has been the least subject to modernization. Here an endless stream of peasants flows into the city, bringing their produce to the market on the backs of their pack animals.

3.3 The Citadel and the Government Quarters

The *qalʿah*, or citadel, which is already mentioned in the earliest Ill. 29 medieval descriptions of Herat, has been destroyed several times.[8] In its present state, the oldest parts date back to the fifteenth century. It consists of a lower-lying barrack section in the west and of a residential and arsenal section in the east. The eastern part was almost completely buried under debris. In the course of recent restoration work, parts of it have been unearthed. As far as one can now see, the eastern part of the *qalʿa* consisted of two courts. Around the western court there was the modest palace of the governor or the commander of the citadel. The buildings east of it apparently served as the arsenal.

In times of peace, the governor of Herat resided not in the *qalʿah* but in the city itself next to the Great Mosque.[9] Here there was a palace consisting of several courts, which is still visible in a photo taken in 1916; Ill. 30 large stables; to the north, a state workshop for the repair of weapons and the production of gunpowder; and farther to the north a big state

39

26. Caravansarai in Herat

27. Caravansarai in Herat

28.   The *ḥouz* near the *chahār-sū* in Herat

29.   The *qalʿah* of Herat

30.   The governor's palace in Herat after Niedermayer

granary. In addition to these buildings there were barracks and stables for the army horses. Of all these buildings only the granary still stands.

3.4. The Great Mosque

The pride of the northeastern quarter of the old city of Herat was, and is, the Friday Mosque. At the beginning of this century it was in a very dilapidated state, but restoration and extension work has been going on for years. The mosque is a typical Iranian four-*īwān* structure. The *īwāns* are flanked by large halls whose vaulted roofs rest on pillars. At the beginning of this century there was, at the north side and adjacent to the mosque, the mausoleum of the Ghūrid Ghiyāth al-Dīn Muḥammad (died 1203), which has since disappeared.[10] There is a Ghūrid inscription above the old southwest portal.[11]

In the second half of the fifteenth century the mosque was completely rebuilt and at this time acquired the basic features of its present shape. I stress "basic features" because a comparison of the present condition of the southwestern part with its state in 1916 reveals that in the course of the restoration the essential character of the building was noticeably changed.

Ill. 31 and 32

42

31. Southeastern part of the Friday Mosque of Herat in 1977

32. Southeastern part of the Friday Mosque of Herat in 1916

3.5. Living Quarters

The residential quarters cover most of the area of the old city of Herat. The access to these residential quarters is provided by four main roads, the bazaar, and by roads constructed parallel to the city walls. (Bazaars were located at the points where the main axes and the lanes of this square meet.) At the request of the British military, in the nineteenth century this square of lanes within the walls and in the south of the *qal'ah* had been broadened and smoothed over.[12] But it already existed before and is part of the original concept which underlies the plan of Herat.

Ill. 33   Off these primary streets of access branch secondary streets which cross the quarters roughly in the north-south and east-west directions. They do not run as straight as is shown on Niedermayer's plan but are somewhat more crooked, as is shown on my mapping. In principle, however, they are clearly articulated.

To say that the plan of these streets in Herat was originally based upon a grid pattern does not appear to me an unfounded interpretation. From the plan of the living quarters, which at first glance appears so tangled, one can detect the same kind of regular ground pattern that we see in Damascus, which is based upon a Hellenistic city plan.[13]

Thus, in the case of Herat, it is inappropriate and misleading to speak of an "organic, irregular plan of the quarters of the old city," and of "streets and lanes narrow and twisting, often subterranean with many sharp turns and frequent cul-de-sacs" as has been recently stated.[14] In Herat, on the contrary, we have a ground plan with four streets which traverse the quarters from east to west and south to north forming small *insulae* (between 10,000 and 15,000 square meters). Also, there were surprisingly few dead-end lanes, which are so common in other Near Eastern cities.

3.6. Religious Buildings

Inside the living quarters in Herat there are many religious buildings: mosques, *ziyārāt* (shrines), and synagogues. Here we are concerned only with Muslim religious buildings.

Without exception the greater mosques of Herat are almost all situated on the fringes of the quarters. The smaller mosques are situated both at the fringe and inside the residential quarters.

The *ziyārāt* are real or presumed tombs of saints, where one prays in the hope of having one's wishes come true or of being healed through the magic power of the saint. They are found in great quantity inside and outside the old city of Herat. In the *Risālah-yi Mazārāt-i Harāt*, a book published in Herat in 1892, almost 300 *ziyārāt* are listed and described. I

33. Map of the inner city of Herat

Ill. 34 know of no other city that could boast of such a high number of shrines. Almost every small group of houses has its own shrine. Some are only small buildings, but others of the *ziyārāt* are larger buildings with several cenotaphs where a sort of neighborhood patron saint is venerated.

Most *ziyārāt* cannot be precisely dated. Their architecture is, in most cases, simple and there are no stylistically distinctive features that might enable us to ascribe them to definite periods. Also, most of the structures have no inscriptions. Nevertheless, for some of them we can arrive at *termini ante quos* denoting them as places of veneration which, of course, might originally have had a different appearance. This is possible when old tombstones or inscriptions can be found in the building or its vicinity,
Ill. 35 or are built into the wall for which a *terminus ante quem* can be established.

3.7. Private Houses

If one climbs up to the remains of the city walls in the southwest
Ill. 36 section of Herat, one can see the plan of some of the private houses. Here, in this part of the city, are relatively simple homes. Their roofs are mostly

34.   A *ziyārāt* in Herat

35. A *ziyārāt* in Herat

flat. Rooms flank inner courtyards on one to four sides. In the courtyards there are gardens, sometimes even a tree which provides shade. Occasionally, wells are also found. Better houses are built with portals which are decorated with terracotta reliefs or tiles and include several courtyards and a large garden.[15]

Ill. 37

Let us take a close look at an old medium-sized house. One enters through a portal and hallway. The hallway is bent in order to block the view from the outside. At the end of the entrance hall there is a wall to provide additional privacy. Only after one has passed this wall can he see the house. The courtyard has been converted into a vegetable garden (and that in the middle of the city and in the vicinity of the Great Mosque!) The main section of the house lies to the north and is comprised of two stories. At the south side of the garden there is another simpler living compound with one story. On the east side there is a

Ill. 38

47

36. View from the southwestern part of the walls of Herat

service compound with rooms for servants, a pantry, and a kitchen. One enters the main section of the house through a stucco-decorated portal by way of a corridor. At the end of the corridor a stairway leads to the upper floor. There is one room on each side of the corridor. The rooms on the ground floor are plain and without decoration. The larger rooms on the Ill. 39 upper floor are quite different. They have large windows overlooking the garden. Their walls are decorated by niches and their ceilings consist of elaborately decorated and executed vaults.

3.8. Sewer Systems

Someone unfamiliar with Near Eastern cities would not guess that a house like the one just described might be found in the stinking lanes littered with refuse.

Ill. 40   Sewer systems, with the exception of the northeast quarter, are unknown in old Herat. Latrines are so placed within the private houses that the pits have openings onto the streets. Waste from the toilets and

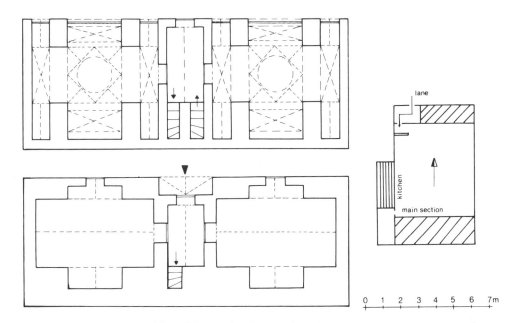

37. Plan of a house in Herat

38. View of a house in Herat

49

39.   Interior of a house in Herat

households collects in small ditches and runs towards sumps called
khandaq. With the exception of the northeastern quarter, which does have
a sewage system, the *khandaqs* are spread all over the city (They are
indicated by dotted areas on Ill. 33.). Some *khandaqs* can be as large as 30
meters in diameter.

Ill. 41

3.9. Conclusion

Let us summarize what we have discovered as the essential features of
the plan of Herat in the nineteenth century. The city walls are square in
shape and oriented to the cardinal points of the compass. They were
constructed on a mound and were protected by an outer ditch. The two
main streets cross in the center of the city, forming the bazaar and the
chahār-sū, and divide it into four equal quarters.

Other streets circle the city just inside the city walls. From these, other
streets, with a few cul-de-sacs, divide the four main quarters of the city
into insulae-like subquarters. The four gates on the main streets are, with

Ill. 42

40.   Lane in Herat

one exception, situated in the middle of the corresponding parts of the city walls. The citadel is located at the edge of the city, but inside the city walls; the Great Mosque is placed near the administrative buildings.

4. MEDIEVAL HERAT

On examining the literary sources on the topography of Herat, we find that the features described above are not only valid for nineteenth-century Herat, but are essential characteristics of medieval Herat as well.

4.1 The Plan According to Tenth-century Sources

The most comprehensive description of the city in the tenth century is found in the books of three Arab geographers, those of Iṣṭakhrī (written around 951), Ibn Ḥawqal (around 977), and Muqaddasī (around 985). Of these Iṣṭakhrī, [16] whom Ibn Ḥawqal follows almost verbatim, offers

41. *Khandaq* in Herat

the best description.[17] Later geographers such as Yāqūt, Qazwīnī, and Mustawfī contribute little. They offer praises but are far less exact than the first three authors.

The following picture of Herat in the tenth century may be drawn from the literary sources. A wall, constructed like all the other buildings in Herat from mud brick, enclosed the city. Its circumference was about 4 kilometers. In front of the wall there was a ditch. Through four gates in the middle of each wall four high roads left the city. The gates faced the four cardinal points of the compass, as they did in nineteenth-century Herat. (Due to construction work in the Tīmūrid period, the direction of the end of the northern axis had been changed.) The road to Balkh passed through the Sarai or Malik gate in the north; the road to Nīshāpūr, through the Ziyād gate in the west; the road to Sīstān, through the Fīrūz-Abād gate in the south; and the road to Ghūr passed through the Khushk gate in the east. With the exception of the Sarai gate, whose doors were of iron, all the other gates had wooden doors. Beginning at each gate a bazaar led into the center of the city.

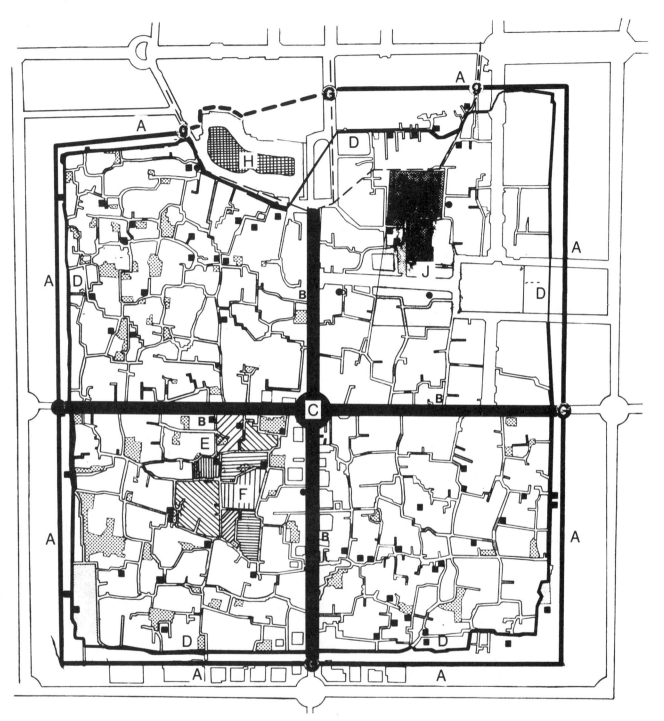

42.   Map of the main elements of the inner city of Herat

The citadel was placed inside the city walls. It was surrounded by double walls and had four gates which were oriented in the same manner as the city gates and bore the same names. There is no doubt that the citadel of medieval times was located where the present one may be found, since the latter stands on a hill overlooking the city.

The location of the Great Mosque, whose oldest components go back to Ghūrid times (the twelfth and thirteenth centuries), certainly did not change between the tenth and the twelfth century. At the turn of the century the administrative complex, the governor's palace, stables, granary, and state workshops lay at the *qibla* of the Great Mosque. The medieval geographers tell us that there was a prison adjacent to the *qibla* of the Great Mosque. Prisons, as a rule, were not erected at random but were generally located where the ruler and his soldiers resided. In Damascus, for example, the old prison was at the *qibla* of the Great Mosque within the governor's compound.[18]

4.2 The Plan According to Fifteenth-century Sources

The fifteenth-century sources, especially Isfizārī, [19] who in 1492 wrote a history of Herat, indicate that the form of the inner city of Herat has remained much the same since the tenth century.

Isfizārī begins his history of Herat with a geographical introduction, on the basis of which the following picture of Herat may be sketched.[20] The circumference of the city walls was 7300 Harātī feet. The distance between opposite gates was 1900 feet (which proves that the city had a square plan). A ditch surrounded the wall. There remained five gates in the wall: in the north, the Malik gate; in the west, the Iraq gate; in the south, the Fīrūz-Abād gate; in the east, the Khushk gate; and in the northeast, the Qīchāq gate. From these gates, with the exception of the Qīchāq gate, bazaars ran to the *chahār-sū* in the center of the city. These bazaars carried the same names as the respective gates. The bazaar in the north, the Malik, the king's bazaar, was built of baked bricks. Thus we may presume that the other bazaars were built of mud bricks.

In each of the bazaars were caravansarais, *tīmhā* as Isfizārī calls them. The Great Mosque was located between the Khushk and the Qīchāq gates at the place which was considered to be sacred and to possess healing qualities. Isfizārī had no precise information about the date of construction of the mosque. He speaks only of an old Kufic inscription from the year 597 (1201). This inscription refers to the same period of construction as the extant inscription mentioned above.

Isfizārī reports that in pre-Timurid times the Kart King Mu'izz al-Dīn (1330-1370), during whose reign the Kart dynasty reached the highest

54

point of its power, surrounded the city with an additional wall measuring about 6 kilometers square. Tīmūr, who had destroyed this wall, did not rebuild it because he considered it impossible to defend.

The evidence presented so far is quite sufficient to draw the following conclusions: Both the plan of the inner city of Herat and the location of the most important buildings—the bazaar, the Great Mosque, the administrative buildings, and the citadel—have undergone only minor changes at most since the tenth century. This permanence distinguishes Herat from other cities of the Irano-Iraqi architectural region, which is characterized by mud and baked brick buildings, and where the location of the central sections of the cities' extensions were often considerably changed through the centuries. The square plan according to which Herat was built has not been found in the plan of other cities of the same size and era west of the two inner Iranian deserts. But we do find it in another Afghani city, Qandahar. This city, however, was founded only in the eighteenth century.

4.3 Origins of the Plan of Herat

How did the particular plan of Herat develop and where should we search for its roots? One thinks immediately of the Greco-Roman cities in western Asia, some of which have rectangular or square plans, two main streets intersecting in the form of a cross in the center, and a secondary network of streets branching off from them. Between the times that these Greco-Roman cities, as well as Byzantine and early Islamic cities which were influenced by them in plan, were built, and the time that Herat was built, a number of Iranian cities were constructed in which we look in vain for the principles of urban design that characterize Herat.

In Iran, however, we encounter small rural settlements with square or rectangular plans, the so-called *qal'ah* settlement. Their similarity with the inner city of Herat, however, is limited to some formal aspects. Because of their much smaller size and the different organizational set-up which shape them, they can only be compared with settlements of the same type in Central Asia.[21]

Qal'ah villages of high antiquity are known in this region.[22] Whereas in Iran there is almost no similarity between the *qal'ah* villages and the cities, in Central Asia we encounter city plans with certain formal similarities with *qal'ah* villages, on the one hand, and structural similarites with Herat, on the other. This, for example is valid for the plan of the Seleucid inner city of Parthian Marv.[23] On the one hand, it is related to the Parthian *qal'ah* settlement of Tobrak-qal'ah by *insulae*, a clearly defined axis, and a citadel at the edge of the city.[24] On the other hand, Marv is related to Herat by the square city wall orientated according to the cardinal points of the compass. (Although a clearly accentuated east-west axis can be seen in Marv, there is no clearly accentuated north-south axis.) Four gates are oriented according to the cardinal points of the compass, through which four overland roads leave the city. In addition, the citadel is located at the northern edge of the city inside the city walls.

West of the old inner city of Marv, a new city of irregular plan arose in the Middle Ages.[25] It had two clearly defined axes. However, here we witness an increasing degeneration of these elements of the plan that resemble Herat. In the fifteenth century we encounter in the city area of Marv a settlement which is differently orientated than its predecessors and which has only one axis.[26]

In three other cities of central Asia, Bukhara,[27] Khiva,[28] and Shakhri Syabz,[29] traces of plans similar to the one of the *madīna* of Herat can still be detected today. In the center of each of the three inner cities (called *shahristān,* the Persian equivalent to the Arab *madīna*) the two main axes of intraurban communication cross. Also, the bazaars of the cities were located at the crossroads. A building, identical with the *chahār-sū* of Herat, the Ṭāq-i Zargarān, was erected at the intersection in Bukhara. In Khiva the citadel is situated inside the walls of the *shahristān* on the west axis. The citadel of Bukhara is to be found adjacent to the *shahristān* in the northwest.

There are some differences with the plan of the inner city of Herat. The *shahristāns* are not orientated precisely according to the cardinal points of the compass, and they are rectangular in Khiva and Shakhri Syabz. Also there was no grid pattern of the streets and lanes. Nevertheless, it is evident that there are close links between Marv, Bukhara, Khiva, and Shakhri Syabz on the one side and Herat on the other. Thus there seems to be ample reason to speak of an eastern Iranian city type which stretches from the southern fringe of the Dasht-i Lūt, east of the Dasht-i Lūt and the Dasht-i Kavīr to the cities of Central Asia.

The question we have to ask now is, does the plan of the inner city of Herat originate from Central Asia or from somewhere else? Since the inner city of Herat represents the Eastern type of city in its purest form, we should consider Herat geographically closer to the point of origin of the principle of urban design we are concerned with here than either Khiva in the north or Bam in the south. That means we must direct our attention to the cultural region to which Herat is the gateway from the west and with which it has been connected culturally for thousands of years, to India.

A search through Indian literature, which is rich in treatises on architecture and urbanism, is rewarding. In the *Mānasāra*, an architectural manual which most scholars date back to the first century B.C., we find the following principles of city planning.[30] The ideal Indian city is orientated in the direction of the cardinal points of the compass. Each city is surrounded by a wall inside of which a citadel is located. Outside the wall there is a ditch. Generally there are four city gates in the middle of each of the four sides. Inside the walls and adjacent to them, wide streets circle the city. In addition, there are two broad streets which connect the opposite gates of the city. They cross each other in the center of the city, where there is a temple or a hall for the inhabitants to congregate. Thus, the city is divided into four quarters each of which is again further divided by lanes. Along the two main streets which cross in the center there are houses, on the ground floors of which there are shops. The rest of the city consists of living quarters.[31] In addition to this, the ideal Indian city is oriented in the direction of the cardinal points of the compass and at the city's fringe, but inside the walls, there is the citadel.[32]

The plan of Herat follows the principles of city planning laid down in this book in seven of its eight characteristic features. Thus, it appears to be more likely that Herat was laid out according to a plan that originated in India, crossed Afghanistan, and reached Central Asia (and also was followed for the *qal'ah* settlements in Iran) than it was from a plan that originated in Central Asia. In order to avoid unrewarding speculation to which research dealing with enquiries into the interference between eastern Hellenistic and Indian cultural and artistic concepts is still restricted to a high degree, I will not ask the question here when Herat first was built following this scheme and how far back in Indian history this scheme goes.[33] There is no question that the geographical position of Herat as well as its history made Indian influence possible. In addition to this, the city belonged in the pre-Islamic period to the Indo-Bactrian cultural sphere, and in Islamic times it was twice ruled by dynasties (Ghaznavids and the Ghūrids) who united parts of eastern Iran and India under their rules.

5. THE SUBURBS OF HERAT

The inner city, the *madīna,* as the Arab geographers called it, stands out by its continuity in plan which may be followed for over a thousand years. The suburbs, called *rabaḍ* by the same geographers, however, were evidently subject to change.

5.1 The Suburbs of Herat in the Tenth Century

From tenth-century literary sources we learn the following about the surrounding area of Herat. The plain north of the city was not under cultivation, and, with the exception of the Nahr al-madīna, there was no water in this plain. To the east and west of the inner city of Herat there were gardens near the gates and, to the south, cultivated land. From the rather scanty reports in the sources, the *extra muros* sections of Herat extended towards the south and might have flanked the inner city in the east and the west. The population density was most likely lower here than in the areas *intra muros*. It is safe to assume a high density of buildings next to the gates in the east, west, and south, as well as along the three overland roads originating there.

Ill. 43

5.2. The Suburbs of Herat from the Tenth to the Fourteenth Centuries

Between the tenth and the fourteenth centuries, the suburbs were developed towards the north. Muʿizz al-Dīn Kart surrounded the considerably extended suburban area with an external wall. In the Kart period (1245-1389) the area covered with buildings around the inner city had grown so much that the old inner city bazaar was no longer sufficient to serve the increased population. Although textual evidence for the existence of bazaars along the overland roads near the gates and of neighborhood bazaars in the suburbs exists only from the fifteenth century, we certainly can assume that such bazaars were there in the pre-Tīmūrid period.

5.3. The Suburbs of Herat in the Fifteenth Century

The Herat of the Tīmūrid period was the undisputed intellectual center of the Iranian cultural sphere. Especially in the second half of the fifteenth century Sulṭān Ḥusain Bāiqarā (died 1507) and his adviser and friend ʿAlī Shīr (died 1501), himself a famous poet, attracted to Herat the outstanding thinkers and artists of their time. The two great historians, Khvāndamīr and Mīrkhvānd, the poet Jāmī and the greatest master of Persian miniature painting, Bihzād, lived at the court of Sulṭān Ḥusain Bāiqarā. Craftsmen from all over Iran and from outside of Iran were gathered here in order to execute the buildings commissioned by the royal family and the grandees of the empire.

In Tīmūrid times the suburbs were extended far beyond the city walls to the north. In the surrounding area there emerged a new intellectual and courtly center with gardens, palaces, mosques, and *madrasas.* In this period, as Isfizārī tells us, bazaars also were established along the four overland roads to the ends of the suburbs.[34] The supplying of the vast

58

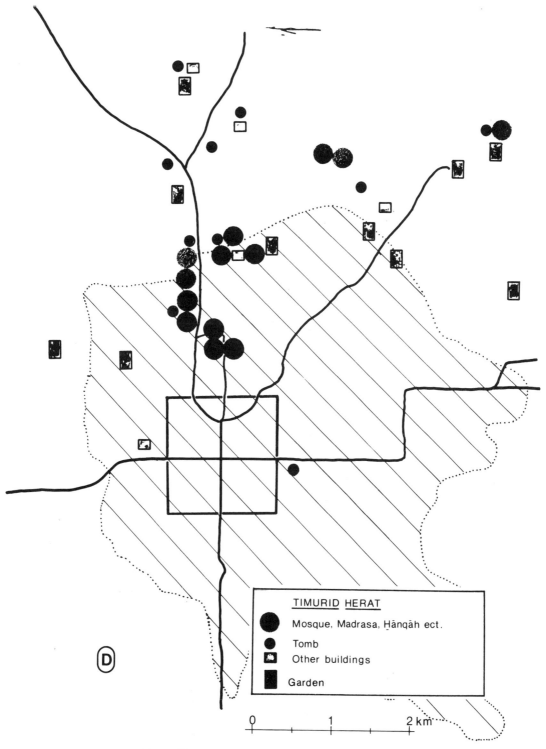

TIMURID HERAT

- ● Mosque, Madrasa, Ḥānqāh ect.
- ● Tomb
- ▣ Other buildings
- ◼ Garden

Ⓓ

0   1   2 km

43. The *extra muros* parts of Herat

living quarters between the overland roads was secured by neighborhood bazaars, as Isfizārī points out.

Khvāndamīr provides us in his chronicle *Khulāṣat al-akhbār* with a long and detailed description of Herat of his day. There he gives us a long list of buildings which at the turn of the fifteenth to the sixteenth centuries were considered to be remarkable.[35]

According to Khvāndamīr, inside the city walls there were seven mosques, eighteen *madrasas*, seventeen *khānqāhs*, four mausoleums, one hospital, and one library. Khvāndamīr likewise mentions the names of fifty-eight buildings outside the city walls and gives descriptions which vary in length. These were fourteen *madrasas*, fourteen mausoleums, twelve mosques, eight *khānqāhs*, three *ribāṭs*, two hospitals, and five other buildings. Though the locations of some of these buildings can be identified, this is not the appropriate place to dwell on them in detail.[36]

In addition to Isfizārī and Khvandamīr, the *Memoirs* of Bābur,[37] the founder of the Indian Moghul dynasty (died 1530), who visited Herat in December of 1506, not long before the rule of the Tīmūrids over Khurasan came to an end, provide us with additional topographic information. Bābur had visited some of his aunts after they had gathered in the *madrasa* of Ḥusain Bāiqarā. From there he went to the *madrasa* of Jawhar Shād where another aunt of his had pitched her tent. There he was wined and dined and lodged. Bābur's own camp was in a garden called the "New Year's garden." This place displeased him and he was then lodged in the former palace of 'Alī Shīr. Several times Bābur visited his two cousins who at that time ruled in Herat and had their residences in the gardens of Jahān Ara and Safīd. From the latter they went to a drinking party in a pavilion which stood in the center of another garden nearby.

This description shows that in Bābur's day the courtly life of Herat took place in the gardens north of the city. In some of these gardens were pavilions, while in other gardens the royal clan lived in elaborate tents, and this even in winter, as Bābur's description shows.

Ill. 44   One of these gardens, the Takht-i Safar, reemerged as a modern park. Although its layout in the fifteenth century was different from what it is today, it gives a good impression of the original appearance of a part of the royal gardens. They were located on the slope of the mountains which border the plain of Herat in the north.

Khvāndamīr devotes a special section of his book to the description of the royal gardens.[38] He reports that his patron, Ḥusain Bāiqarā, began to extend the number of gardens around Herat. His most favored gardens were situated to the northeast of the city where the air was very pure and

60

44.   The garden Takht-i Safar near Herat

the water was very good. The construction of the Jahān Arā garden was carried out with great effort. In addition to this garden, Khvāndamīr mentions four more which were laid out by Ḥusain Bāiqarā. All had beautiful pavilions and other buildings. 'Alī Shīr imitated his master and friend in also laying out gardens and garden pavilions. Khvāndamīr mentions nine more gardens that were laid out in the time of Ḥusain Bāiqarā.

Gardens, above all those of Samarqand, the capital of Tīmūr, and of Herat, are one of the important manifestations of cultural change that took place in the Tīmūrid period. Although rulers of Iran in pre-Tīmūrid times resided in gardens outside the cities, the Tīmūrids lived in suburbs with wide areas covered by gardens, palaces, and sacred buildings. These suburbs differed decisively from the suburbs of earlier periods, which were merely organic extensions of the inner cities brought on by economic and demographic changes. The Tīmūrid garden suburbs differ also from the garden quarters of pre-Tīmūrid times, for example those of eleventh-century Isfahan.[39]

The Tīmūrid garden suburbs are the expression of a new way of life which originated in the nomadic milieu but which was soon transformed into courtly refinements for which Herat is a good example. Bābur and Clavijo, the Castilian ambassador to Tīmūr in Samarqand, portray the life of the royal clan outside the city walls.[40] Also, the painter Bihzād has captured it in the miniatures he painted in Herat.[41]

61

In 1510 the Uzbeks lost Khurasan and with it Herat to the Ṣafavids, under whom the city experienced a brief cultural revival. This, however, petered out towards the end of the sixteenth century because most of the artists and scholars emigrated to the new royal residences of Tabriz, Qazvin, and Bukhara.[43] None of these cities succeeded in equaling Herat in splendor.

Only in Isfahan did ʿAbbās I, who was born in Herat in 1571, create a new cultural center which towered over all other cities of Iran. And as in Herat under the Tīmūrids, the courtly life of Ṣafavid Isfahan took place in the gardens which ʿAbbās had laid out at the periphery of his new capital.

Here the new urbanistic concept introduced in Samarqand and Herat found its fulfillment. In contradistinction to the Tīmūrids and earlier rulers under whom the planning of the garden suburbs was executed piecemeal, ʿAbbās subjected all his buildings to a coherent master conception, which went far beyond the old limits of Isfahan and affected much of the natural features of the landscape around the city.

NOTES

1. L. W. Adamec (ed.), *Herat and North-western Afghanistan (Historical and Political Gazetteer of Afghanistan*, vol. 3) (Graz, 1975), 152 and 160.

2. The most instructive of their works are A. Conolly, *Journey to the North of India* (London, 1834); J. P. Ferrier, *Caravan Journeys and Wandering in Persia, Afghanistan, Turkestan, and Beluchistan* (London, 1856); A. Hamilton, *Afghanistan* (London, 1906); N. Khanikoff, "Lettre à M. Reinaud," *Journal Asiatique 5e série*, 15 (1860), 537-543; M. M. Lal, "A Brief Description of Herat," *Journal of the Asiatic Society of Bengal*, 3 (1834), 9-18; G. B. Malleson, *Herat. The Granary and Garden of Central Asia* (London, 1880); O. v. Niedermayer, *Afghanistan* (Leipzig, 1924); A. Vambèry, *Travels in Central Asia* (London, 1864); C. E. Yates, "Notes on the City of Herát," *Journal of the Asiatic Society of Bengal*, 56 (1887), 84-106.

3. A. Conolly, *op. cit.*, 121.

4. O. v. Niedermayer, *op. cit.*, plan 3.

5. This description is based mainly on L. W. Adamec, *op. cit.*, 160-163 and 174-179.

6. Map of Herat, drawn by C. F. North, Fort Williams 1842.

7. See below

8. See below

9. See ill. 24.

10. Cf. O. v. Niedermayer, *op. cit.*, 55, fig. 4.

11. N. Hatch Wolf, *Herat. A Pictorial Guide* (Kabul, 1966), 22f.

12. L. W. Adamec, *op. cit.*, 179.

13. Cf. E. Wirth, "Die orientalische Stadt. Ein Uberblick aufgrund jüngerer Forschungen zur materiellen

Kultur," *Saeculum,* 26 (1975), 45-94, fig. 6

14. P. English, "The Traditional City of Herat. Afghanistan," L. C. Brown (ed.), *From Madina to Metropolis* (Princeton, 1973), 73-90, 78.

15. Cf. R. Samizay, "Herati housing of Afghanistan," *Ekistics,* 38 (No. 227, Oct. 1974), 247-251.

16. al-Istakhrī, Ibrāhīm b. Muhammad, *Kitāb masālik al-mamālik,* (ed.) M. al-Hīnī (Cairo, 1961), 149-151.

17. Ibn Hawqal, Abū 'l-Qāsim b. Hasan, *Kitāb sūrat al-ard* (Beirut, n.d.), 366.

18. N. Elisséef, *La description de Damas d'Ibn ʿAsākir,* (Damascus, 1959), 39.

19. Isfizārī, Muʿīn al-Dīn Muhammad, *Rawdāt al-jannāt fi ansāf Harāt,* (ed.) M. K. Imām (Tehran, 1338/1960.).

20. Isfizārī, *op. cit.,* 77-79.

21. G. Kortum, "Ländliche Siedlungen im Umland von Shiraz," R. Stewig and H. G. Wagner (ed.), *Kulturgeographische Untersuchungen im islamischen Orient* (Schriften des Geographischen Instituts der Universität Kiel, Band 38) (Kiel, 1973), 177-212.

22. E. E. Nerasik, *Sel'skije poseleniya afrigidskogo Choresma* (Moscow, 1966).

23. G. A. Pugatschenkowa and L. I. Rempel, *Istoriya iskusstv Uzbekistana* (Moscow, 1965), fig. 10.

24. G. A. Pugatschenkowa, *Puti raswitija architektury juschnogo Turkmenistana pory rabowladenija i feodalisma* (Moscow, 1958), 42.

25. G. A. Pugatschenkowa, *op. cit.,* 191.

26. G. A. Pugatschenkowa, *op. cit.,* 382.

27. W. A. Lavrov, *Gradostroitelnaya kultura srednei Asii* (Moscow, 1950), fig. 28 and 29.

28. W. A. Lavrov, *op. cit.,* fig. 41.

29. Masson, M. E. and G. A. Pugatschenkova, "Shakhri Syabz pri Tim-
ure i Ulug Beke", *Iran,* 16, 103-126, 115.

30. P. K. Acharya, *Architecture of Mānasāra* (Mānasāra series VI) (London, 1934).

31. D. N. Shukla, *Vāstū-Sāstra* (Chandigarh, n.d.), I, 247-248.

32. D. N. Shukla, *op. cit.,* I, 582; G. Niemeier, *Siedlungsgeographie* (Braunschweig, 1972), 144.

33. Cf. D. Schlumberger, "Descendants non-méditerranéens de l'art grec," *Syria,* 3 (1960), 131-166 and 253-318.

34. Isfizārī, *op. cit.,* 78.

35. D. Price, *Mohammedan History* (London, 1821), III, 641-656.

36. Cf. H. Gaube, "Innenstadt—Aussenstadt. Kontinuität und Wandel im Grundriss von Herāt (Afghanistan) zwischen dem X. und dem XV. Jahrhundert," G. Schweizer (ed.), *Beiträge zur Geographie orientalischer Städte und Märkte* (Beihefte zum Tübinger Atlas des Vorderen Orients, Reihe B, Nr. 24) (Wiesbaden, 1977), 213-240, 227-231

37. Bābur, Zāhir al-Dīn Muhammad, *Bābur-nāma (The Bābur-nāma in English . . . transl. . . . by A. S. Beveridge)* (²London, 1969), 301-306.

38. D. Price, *op. cit.,* 654-656.

39. Cf. Māfarrūkhī, Mufaddal b. Saʿd, *Kitāb mahāsin Isfahān,* (ed.) J. al-Husainī (Tehran 1312/1933), 53-80.

40. R. G. de Clavijo, *Narrative of the Embassy of Ruy Gonzales de Clavijo to the Court of Timour at Samarcand A.D. 1403-6* (The Hakluyt Society. First Series No. XXVI) (²New York, 1970).

41. E.g. the representation of the garden Jahān-Arā on a miniature kept in the Golestan Museum, Tehran. Cf. D. N. Wilber, *Persian Gardens and Garden Pavilions* (Rutland/Tokyo 1962), 62 f.

42. Cf. V. Minorsky: *Calligraphers and Painters* (Washington, 1959), 31f.

CHAPTER THREE

Isfahan—The Capital

1. INTRODUCTION

The Persians say: *"Isfahān niṣf-i jahān,"* "Isfahan is the half of the world." And although their language is not poor in rhetorical figures, there is no comparable old saying about any other Iranian city. In fact, no other Iranian city has shown such a stubborn will to live as Isfahan, which in the course of its history was several times destroyed and rebuilt.

The city is located halfway between the Caspian Sea and the Persian Gulf. Next to Tehran it is the second largest city of Iran, the seat of major industrial enterprises, an important commercial city, and a city with two and a half millennia of history.

1.1. Situation of Isfahan

At first glance, it appears to be anything but obvious that a large settlement should have been developed at the place that Isfahan was located in the course of millennia. As opposed to the large Iranian cities of Tabriz, Tehran, and Mashhad, which are situated in or at the edge of vast, well-watered agricultural provinces, or to the cities on the west Iranian mountain rim, Kirmanshah and Hamadan, which are favored with abundant precipitation, Isfahan, situated at an elevation of 1500 meters, is a city surrounded by deserts and semi-deserts. Here, in a basin of the central Iranian mountain chain, settlement and agricultural activities are possible only at a few spots favored by nature. The essential precondition for agriculture and urban growth in such a situation is a sufficient water supply. This is provided to Isfahan and its hinterland by the Zāyandah-Rūd, which has the most abundant water flow of all the rivers of the land-locked Iranian interior. With the minimal flow of around 30 cubic meters per second, the Zāyandah-Rūd is the basis of existence of the city. It provides both the water for the irrigation of the fields around the city and the drinking water for its people. In this, Isfahan resembles three other oasis cities, which, like it, have played important roles in Islamic history, Damascus in Syria, Herat in Afghanistan, and Samarqand in Uzbekistan.

Although Isfahan actually is favored by nature, it did not become, by itself alone, a center towering over other Iranian cities. Its location, almost midway between the two great emporia of Damascus and Aleppo in the west and Samarqand and Bukhara in the east, made it a center for the exchange of goods and ideas from the east and west of the Islamic world. Its central position in Iran predestined it to become the capital of the empire under two mighty dynasties.

1.2. Importance of Isfahan

These two functions, the one as emporium, the other as capital, manifested themselves in the bazaar and in the courtly buildings which gave Isfahan the reputation of an oriental Versailles.

As an original creation of the Islamic Middle Ages, the bazaar is the primary characteristic of the Islamic oriental city, and clearly distinguishes the Islamic oriental city from the cities of all other civilizations and other historical periods. In the bazaar, trade, crafts, and banking are organizationally entwined. Its lanes, which are to a large extent vaulted, are lined by shops and workshops of retail merchants and craftsmen, halls in which precious goods are sold, and caravansarais and yards serving the wholesale and long-distance trade, all of which form a spatial contiguity and an architectural whole.[1] The development of the bazaar and city are everywhere in the Islamic world closely related, but in Isfahan we notice an extraordinarily high degree of mutual connection. If one wants to investigate the growth of the one, one must also look closely at the growth of the other.

Thus, it seems appropriate here to treat the development of the city of Isfahan in a chronological order. In doing this we must answer so many fundamental and controversial questions that we can only occasionally dwell on this or that detail. The topics which most concern us here are the vital arteries of the city, the main routes of intraurban communication, in other words, the bazaars as well as other influences that

66

determine location. We must isolate these influences and examine their imprint on the city's development up to the seventeenth century. The periods following the seventeenth century and the spectacular changes taking place today must remain beyond the scope of our discussion.

2. DEVELOPMENT OF ISFAHAN UP TO THE EIGHTH CENTURY

Since no archeological work has been done in Isfahan, we can only speculate about the location of Gabae/Aspadana, the Achaemenid predecessor of the later Isfahan.[2] In the post-Achaemenid centuries, this place is mentioned in literary sources under the name of Aspahān.[3] This settlement was most probably located at the place of present-day Isfahan since (from the fourth century A.D.) two capitals from the sixth and seventh centuries were found within Isfahan. Asfahān or Isfahan is mentioned as an episcopal seat in Nestorian synodal acts from the Sasanian period (the third to the seventh century A.D.).[4] Also, the abbreviation ASP for Aspahān appears on Sasanian coins from the fourth century onward.[5]

2.1. Yahūdiyya and Jayy

The first to provide us with information which enables us to form an idea of how Isfahan developed up to the tenth century A.D. are Arab geographers and historians who wrote at the time and later. According to these sources, the Muslim Arabs conquered the region around Isfahan in the middle of the seventh century A.D. They encountered two cities, Yahūdiyya ("the Jewish city") and Jayy. Yahūdiyya is the ancestor of present-day Isfahan, while only a few ruins, a debris mound, and a medieval bridge over the Zāyandah-Rūd, about 8 kilometers southeast from the center of present-day Isfahan, bear witness to ancient Jayy.

The Arab authors who, when dealing with the pre-Islamic history of Iran, had used middle-Persian chronicles and documents which have since disappeared, considered Yahūdiyya the older of the two cities. Its Jewish population, whose descendents still live in Isfahan, trace their origins back to the time of the Babylonian captivity.[6]

Information which provides us with some vague ideas of the shape of Jayy is preserved in the works of the Arab geographers of the tenth century and in those of two authors of the eleventh century, Māfarrūkhī, who wrote a glorification of Isfahan,[7] and Abū Nu'aim. The latter, who died in 1038, wrote a history of the scholars and outstanding personalities of Isfahan, the *Akhbār Iṣbahān*.[8] This work contains a lengthy historical and topographical introduction, the best source for the topography of pre-and early Islamic Isfahan.

Some traditions mentioned in this work date the founding of Jayy back to legendary times before Alexander the Great, and others, to Alexander's own day. Other traditions, likewise to be found in Abū Nu'aim's book, are more credible. They attribute the founding of Jayy to the two Sasanian Shahs Pērōz, 459-486 A.D., and Khosrō I, 531-579 A.D.[9] Further, we learn from Abū Nu'aim that Sasanian Jayy was not continuously inhabited but served as a fortified refuge for the inhabitants of the neighbouring unfortified settlements.[10]

(The opinion occasionally put forward that Jayy was a "typically Sasanian round city" cannot be proved on the basis of the literary sources.[11] Indeed, there is even more evidence that the typical Sasanian city was not round at all but had quite another shape, as has already been pointed out.

Jayy had four gates, the Bāb Khūr, Bāb Asfīs, Bāb Tīra and Bāb Yahūdiyya. Their locations were determined by certain seasonal positions of the sun.)[12] As far as the extension and the number of towers in the wall of Jayy is concerned, Abū Nu'aim gives contradictory information. This is due to the fact that he quotes different sources one after the other without critical evaluation. In his time, at the beginning of the eleventh century,—and he is not necessarily referring to Sasanian Jayy—the walls of the city had irregular contours. This can be seen on the basis of the measurements Abū Nu'aim provides. The most coherent series of measurements we find in his book had been supplied to him by the mathematician Muḥammad ibn Lurra.[13] He states the circumference of Jayy to be 7100 *dhira'* (1 *dhira'* varies from 0.6 to 0.8 meters). The city was 1752 *dhira'* wide and 1500 long. The distribution of gates in the wall and the number of towers in its different sections were as irregular as the shape of the wall. The distance between the gates varies, as does the number of towers in the individual sections. The number of towers between the individual gates was eighteen to thirty-five. Altogether there were 100 towers in the walls of Jayy.

Inside the city walls Khosrō I (531-579) had constructed some buildings. Ibn Rustah, an Arab geographer who wrote around 903, mentions an old citadel in Jayy.[14] According to Ibn al-Nadīm (ca. 987) some old Pahlavi manuscripts were found there, and this would suggest that we should think of Sasanian Jayy not only as a fortified refuge but also as an administrative center of its hinterland.[15] Further evidence for this is the existence of the Maidān al-Sūq, the marketplace, mentioned

68

by both Abū Nuʿaim [16] and Māfarrūkhī.[17] This *maidān* was located in front of the Khūr gate, in the north of Jayy.

The location of this market is of importance because it proves that already in early times—and I do not hesitate to say in pre-Islamic times—there was a marketplace near the gate for which a special open space, a *maidān*, was provided. Most probably the peasants or farmers of the hinterland of Jayy met at this *maidān* in pre- and early Islamic times. This again underlies the central function the city had for its hinterland. Up to the tenth century the population of Isfahan went out every year to the Maidān as-Sūq to celebrate the New Year. In connection with this festival a yearly fair came to take place regularly. The Būyid Aḍud al-Dawla (949-982) was so pleased with it that he set up a similar fair in Shiraz.[18]

After the Muslim conquest of Iran, the Arabs built their first Friday Mosque in the region of Isfahan at Jayy.[19] The decision to build the mosque in Jayy rather than in Yahūdiyya was governed by rational and strategic reasons. Due to its fortifications and the open spaces enclosed within the wall, areas which in Sasanian times served to shelter refugees in times of war and insecurity, Jayy was most fitted to served the Arabs as a military camp. In the course of stabilization of the political conditions in Iran and the growing amalgamation between Arabs and Iranians, Jayy lost its importance as a garrison of the conquerors.

2.2. Kushīnān

Shortly after 767 the seat of the governor was transferred from fortified Jayy to Khusīnān, a village situated between Jayy and Yahūdiyya. Here the governor, Ayyūb b. Ziyād, erected a palace and opposite to it a Friday Mosque on the bank of the Nahr Fursān, a canal which can no longer be precisely located.[20] Some place this mosque on the site of the present Shaʿyā Mosque, [21] which I can neither support nor refute.

In addition to these two structures, Ayyūb ordered the construction of a large bazaar on the outskirts of Khusīnān facing in the direction of Yahūdiyya. Along with this government-sponsored program, extensive private buildings were constructed. Soon the houses of Khushīnān became contiguous with those of Yahūdiyya.[22]

2.3. Kushīnān and Yahūdiyya

Having grown together with Yahūdiyya, Khushīnān was forced to compete with this city in order to maintain its own position as the administrative and religious center of the region. The new bazaar did help Khushīnān attract people and goods and make Islamic Khushīnān the economic center of the new urban unit. Some cities founded by the Moslems with the same aims and under similar conditions succeeded in becoming such centers. Khushīnān did not.[23] Islamic Khushīnān was not only unable to thwart the growth of Yahūdiyya and direct all urban and building activities to the southeast, but Yahūdiyya, the Jewish town, was at this period already so filled with pulsating life that eventually it absorbed Khushīnān. As early as 773 this process was so advanced that a new Friday Mosque, the third in the region of Isfahan, began to be built in Yahūdiyya on the location of the present day Friday Mosque of Isfahan.[24]

2.4. Jayy and Yahūdiyya

The transfer of the center of activity in the area of Isfahan from Jayy to Yahūdiyya is confirmed by numismatic evidence. There are coins struck between 695 and 746 with the mintmark of Jayy, whereas all later coins bear the mintmark of Isfahan.[25]

The Arab geographers of the tenth century describe Jayy simply as a small village in the region of Isfahan about which they tell all kinds of old legends and of whose former importance they are aware. They describe Yahūdiyya, however, as the most important place of the region of Isfahan. They describe its *madīna*, with the large Friday Mosque in the center of a bustling bazaar, which was visited daily by large crowds of people with wares from kingdoms far and near.[26]

3. THE DEVELOPMENT OF ISFAHAN UP TO 1500

3.1. Sources

Our discussion of the development of Isfahan up to the eighth century had to be of a somewhat general nature. There are no concrete topographic data, since no archeological work has yet been done in Jayy. However, from the time that the urban center was transferred to Yahūdiyya, that is, to the center of the present-day city of Isfahan, a decisive change took place. In addition to the literary sources, we now have as further important evidence the basic shape of the city's plan, and, to a lesser degree, some buildings. Only a small number of dated buildings from the period before 1500 (the period with which we are

Ill. 51 concerned) have been preserved in Isfahan. The basic shape of the city's plan, however, allows us to draw precise conclusions for the period before 1500 as well.

3.2. The Plan of Isfahan

(As I pointed out in the first chapter, the plan of oriental cities, as a rule—to which Isfahan is no exception—consists of A) the main axes of intra-urban communication which connect the city center with the gates and give access to the residential quarters; B) there are the twisted dead-end lanes which give access to individual buildings or groups of buildings. A geographical analysis of the main features of the city's plan reveals that in Isfahan three ground plans have been used, characterized by different orientations of their main axes. They reflect each of the three important periods of the growth of the city.[27]

Ill. 45

Within the oldest of these ground patterns, which is characterized by roads running from southwest to northeast and from southeast to northwest, are to be found both the Friday Mosque and the old *maidān*. The area characterized by this ground pattern stretches out beyond the Friday Mosque to the northeast. Here, most probably, we can locate pre-Islamic Yahūdiyya. Adjacent is the area of the earliest Islamic building period which stretches out to the southwest, south, and northwest of the Friday Mosque.)

3.3. The Great Mosque

As already mentioned, the construction of the Friday Mosque was begun in 773. Of this building, and of the structure rebuilt in the tenth century, nothing remains above ground.

In the present-day structure of the Friday Mosque five individual periods of building activity and several restoration phases can be identified.[28] The courtyard facades were redesigned between the fourteenth and the seventeenth centuries. Since then the ceramic decorations have been continuously restored. Behind these facades we find entire sections of the building which can be clearly identified as belonging to specific building periods. The domed structure in the north, the Gunbad-i Khākī, was built in 1089 by the order of the vizier Tāj al-Mulk, a rather sinister figure at the court of the Saljūqs. Almost contemporary with it and similar in style is the large domed structure above the *miḥrāb* opposite the Gunbad-i Khākī at the south side of the mosque. Almost all of the halls surrounding the courtyard were built in the first half of the twelfth century. At that time, following extensive fire damage, an almost entirely new mosque had to be built. In the course of this construction work the hall-mosque was transformed into a four-*īwān* structure, which since then has been the typical style of the Iranian mosque.

Ill. 46

Ill. 46,1

Ill. 46,2

Ill. 46,3

Between 1366 and 1376 a new prayer hall was built in the northeast section of the mosque, facing a stucco *miḥrāb* dated 1310. The partly

Ill. 46,4

71

1. Oldest street patterns of Islamic Isfahan
2. Street patterns of tenth century Isfahan
3. Street patterns from era of Shah ᶜAbbâs

45. The three ground patterns of the streets in Isfahan

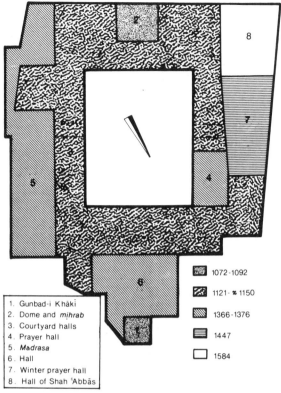

1. Gunbad-i Khāki
2. Dome and *miḥrab*
3. Courtyard halls
4. Prayer hall
5. *Madrasa*
6. Hall
7. Winter prayer hall
8. Hall of Shah ʿAbbās

1072-1092
1121- 1150
1366-1376
1447
1584

46.   The main building periods of the
Friday-Mosque of Isfahan

destroyed *madrasa* at the east side of the mosque dates from the same   Ill. 46,5
period, as does the hall south of the Gunbad-i Khākī. The last two
construction periods of the Friday Mosque of Isfahan fall in the fifteenth   Ill. 46,6
and the sixteenth centuries. Behind the west *īwān* a winter prayer hall   Ill. 46,7
was built in 1447. This hall has a northern continuation in a hall built in
1584 under Shāh ʿAbbās the Great.   Ill. 46,8

3.4. The Old *Maidān*

The old *maidān* is the other important element in the layout of   Ill. 48
medieval Isfahan. Today, this square is built over with simple workshops
and warehouses. In the north it is used as a fruit and vegetable market.
The bazaar in the northwest, the Bāzār-i Shāh, is a part of the bazaar
main axis between the new *maidān* in the southwest and the Friday
Mosque in the northeast. It is roughly aligned with the Saljūqid
southeast wall of the Friday Mosque. Thus we may suppose that it
follows the alignment of the bazaar which already existed in the twelfth
century.

47.   View of the Friday Mosque of Isfahan

The Bāzār-i Rīsmān is located on the northeastern border of the old *maidān*. Today wide stretches of this bazaar are covered with wooden roofs. In former times it was covered entirely by vaults. A *terminus ante quem* for its construction is provided by an inscription dated 1640.[29] In this bazaar is found the Madrasa Kāsah-Garān, the "Potters' *Madrasa*," dated 1694.[30] This *madrasa* was most probably built on the site of another *madrasa* erected a hundred years earlier by Shāh Tahmāsp (1524-1576).[31] Since there is no pre-Safavid building in this area it is possible that in the Middle Ages the *maidān* stretched farther to the northeast and reached the immediate vicinity of the Friday Mosque.

Towards the southwest, the old *maidān* is bordered by a road, which was part of a nineteenth-century extension of the shrine Hārūn Vilāyat, dated 1513.[32] The facade of this shrine formed the seventeenth-century border of the old *maidān*. This building most probably stands at the site of a much older construction. Thus, we may suppose that the medieval southwest edge of the old *maidān* lay very near the facade of Hārūn Vilāyat.

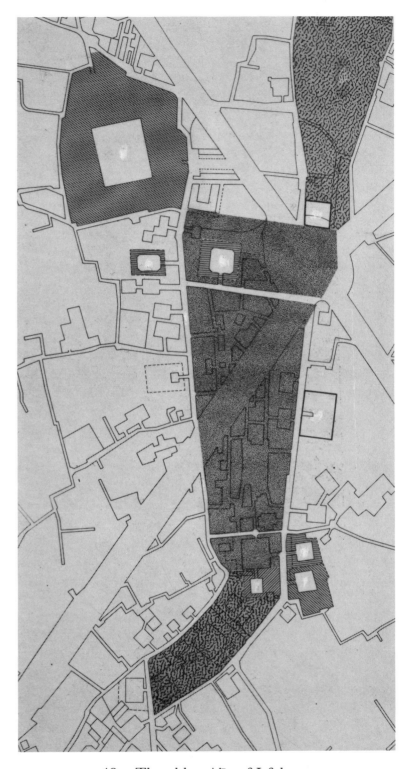

48.   The old *maidān* of Isfahan

On the southeast, finally, the old *maidān* was bordered by another alley which had to give way to a modern through street. At the southeast side there are three Ṣafavid buildings, among them the ʿAlī-mosque, built around 1515.[33] In the northwestern corner of this mosque there is a Saljūqid minaret built into the structure. This minaret marks the medieval southeast border of the old *maidān*.

The old *maidān* was surrounded by mosques, *madrasas*, palaces, an elaborate bazaar, the *Qaiṣariyyah*, and a royal music pavilion, the *Naqqārah-Khānah*. Most of these buildings could still be seen in the seventeenth century, albeit in ruinous condition.[34]

3.5. The Development of the Old *Maidān*

Since the old *maidān* of Isfahan is the prototype of the new *maidān*, built at the beginning of the seventeenth century by Shāh ʿAbbās I, we should assign to it a central role in our discussion of the development of the city of Isfahan. There is no other extant medieval structure in Iran similar to the old *maidān* of Isfahan, nor do we find descriptions of this *maidān* or similar structures in the medieval literature. Thus it is not surprising that there are contradicting opinions concerning its date of origin and the process of its formal articulation. To resolve these contradictions one should perhaps begin by posing two important questions. First, why does the old *maidān* lie in the center of the old city of Isfahan, and, second, why did it become the administrative and religious center of the city?

We can arrive at the answers to these questions by examining the meaning of the term *maidān* in general and by exploring the origins and the development of the old *maidān* of Isfahan in particular.

A *maidān* was originally a horse-race course. The word *maidān* is itself of Iranian origin and has a Persian synonym in *asprēs*.[35] In the compound form, *maidān asfrīs* (*-asprēs*), both words can be found in medieval Arabic literature as the name of the old *maidān* of Isfahan.[36] More generally, however, *maidān* means a place, square. It is likely, then, that the place before the Khūr Gate in Jayy was called Maidān al-Sūq. We do not know whether in Jayy horse races took place on this site. This is conceivable, but it is also possible that in Jayy there was a special race course, since the name of one of the gates of Jayy, the Bāb Asfīs, looks like a corrupted form of Bāb Asfrīs, which would mean "The Hippodrome Gate." [37] *Maidāns* were located on the outskirts of many Iranian and Iraqi cities, serving as horse racing courses and polo fields. We have literary evidence from the ninth century that *maidāns* were used as polo fields. Also, in the west, for example in Damascus and Aleppo, there were *maidāns* in the Middle Ages.[38] That race courses were the ideal sites for markets (cf. Maidān al-Sūq) and for trade is obvious, since horse races did not take place every day. There is abundant literary evidence from the Middle Ages proving the commercial exploitation of these *maidāns*.[39]

Up to the eighth century, the old *maidān* of Isfahan was located at the edge of the settlement. Thus, there is no reason not to date its origin back into pre-Islamic times. But a decisive change took place as a consequence of the eighth-century building activities in Khushīnān. According to Abū Nu'aim houses were built around Khushīnān until they reached those of Yahūdiyya.[40] As a result of the new construction activity, the *maidān* was no longer at the outskirts of Yahūdiyya but in the center of the new urban unit formed by Yahūdiyya and Khushīnān (which in the tenth century went under the name of Yahūdiyya). Here, at the northwest side of the *maidān*, the Friday Mosque was built in the eighth century. Then,

Ill. 49

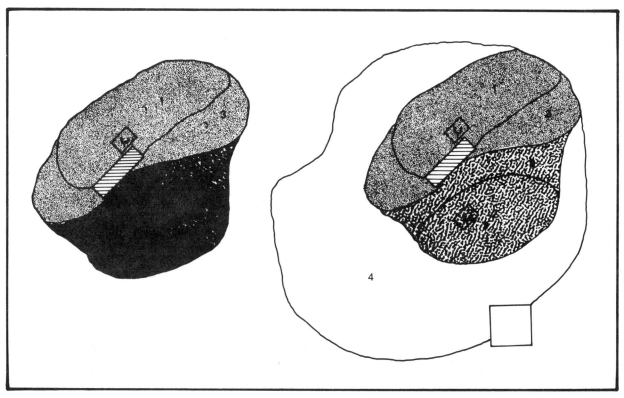

49. The development of Khushīnān and Yahūdiyya (scheme). Phase 1 represents Yahūdiyya with the *maidān* at the outskirts, as it was in the beginning of the eighth century. Phase 2 depicts the nucleus of Khushīnān. Phase 3 shows the expansion of Yahūdiyya and Khushīnān as they developed in the course of their amalgamation. Phase 4, finally, shows the contours of the tenth-century city.

in the course of extensive building activity that took place in the eleventh century in all these areas which are characterized by the second street scheme, the old *maidān* became definitely and for a long time to follow the undisputed center of the city.[41] Engelbert Kaempfer, a German traveler who visited Isfahan in 1684, stresses the central position of the old *maidān* in describing it as *"Forum antiquum in media urbe veteri."*[42]

In the eleventh century at the latest, when Isfahan was the capital of the mighty Saljūq empire, the old *maidān's* original functions as a sports and commercial site were supplemented by a third function brought about by its central location: It became the religious and administrative center of the city.

The old *maidān* remained as the center of the city until the sixteenth century. Then, the new *maidān* was built, which was modeled after the old *maidān*. The new *maidān* became the administrative center of the city and attracted much of the trade, especially that in highly valued goods. The old *maidān* continued to exist, however, as the second center of Isfahan. Today it is still evident that the main axes of intra-urban communication of the pre-motorized age converge from the periphery of the city on the

Ill. 50   magnet of the old *maidān,* and not on its later competitor, the new *maidān.*

3.6. The Main Gates and Roads of Isfahan

These main axes of intraurban communication were those of the Middle Ages, for if they were more recent, they would not converge onto the old but onto the new *maidān*. In the tenth century wall the most important of the city gates were situated along these axes. The putative locations of some of them are marked on Ill. 50. A detailed inquiry into the location of all medieval gates, however, as it had been attempted by some, seems to me an unrewarding enterprise. Even the most complicated and strenuous attempts to extrapolate on the basis of very disparate material produce results that are of necessity wrought with uncertainty, doubt, and disorder. This must not surprise us at all since already in the seventeenth century the medieval city gates no longer had any function. The city had grown beyond the medieval walls, and the Ṣafavids did not defend their empire at the gates of their capital but at its extreme borders, be they in Central Asia or in Iraq. The four main axes of old Isfahan indicated on Ill. 50 were still, at the beginning of this century, lined for long stretches with shops and workshops, forming the bazaar of the city.[43] That they are of high antiquity is also shown by the fact that, on account of the sediment collected over the centuries, they run from 1 to 2 meters above the level of the courtyards on both sides of them. In

1974, excavations for a new sewage system were carried on in the southwestern part of the bazaar of Isfahan, and there one could see that below the surface of the lanes there was a layer of debris 4 meters thick. Along these great roads linear bazaars had already been built by the tenth century.[44] Those in the north and northwest, the Bāzār-i Majlisī and the Bāzār-i Dar-Dasht are still partly preserved. The road running from the west gate in a northeastern direction became, after 1600, part of the main bazaar axis. It was joined by a street that came from the south gate which around the year 1000 lay close to the intersection of the two, but which in pre-Ṣafavid times was located further to the south. Another bazaar was located toward the east of the old *maidān,* called the Bāzār-i Ghāz which was destroyed with the cutting through of Kh. Riżā Pahlavī. At the northeast corner of the old *maidān* are the vestiges of another bazaar which can be clearly distinguished on a 1924 map and on old aerial photographs.[45] We may consider it to be the old Qaiṣariyyah *"le vieux marché imperial,"* of which Chardin speaks in the seventeenth century.[46]

There is no recognizable road leading from the old *maidān* toward the southeast. There are two possible reasons that we cannot locate a main road through this section of the city: Either everything had been totally destroyed in late medieval times, or the density of the population in the area between the old *maidān* and the *qal‘ah* was never as great as it was elsewhere and a road was not needed. The latter reason is more probable. Literary sources allow us to conclude that here, in the Islamic new city of Isfahan, there stood a number of religious buildings (especially *madrasas*) and large mansions with gardens.[47] (The latter structures were *intra muros* and were the equivalents of the great gardens with their palaces south of the city near the river, of which Māfarrūkhī speaks at length but gives us almost no topographic information.[48] A seventeenth-century traveler, J. Thévenot, wrote that the southeastern part of the city was rebuilt in Ṣafavid times and that earlier there had been gardens (in the place of medieval buildings). Such extensive usage of the southeastern parts of the city did not necessitate a main axis between the citadel and the old *maidān* in the Middle Ages. In the late Ṣafavid period, when Thévenot wrote, such a route could no longer be developed because the flow of goods and pedestrians had already been pulled to the southwest, in the direction of the new *maidān.*

Through the determination of the main routes of intraurban communication and their intersection point, the old *maidān,* all those parts of the medieval city which formed its skeleton are isolated.

Here originated the central bazaar area round the old *maidān* to whose

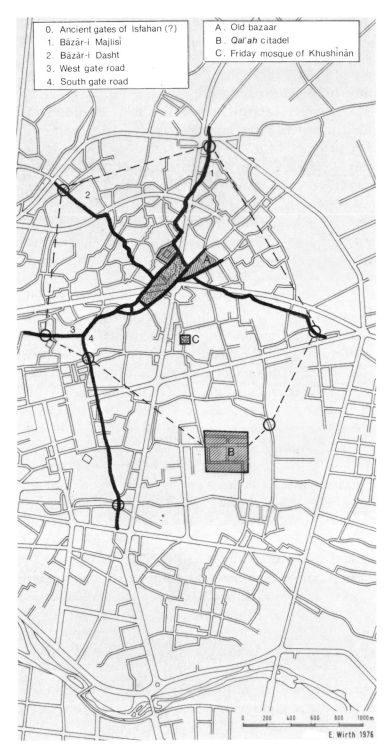

50. The main axes of intra urban communication in old Isfahan

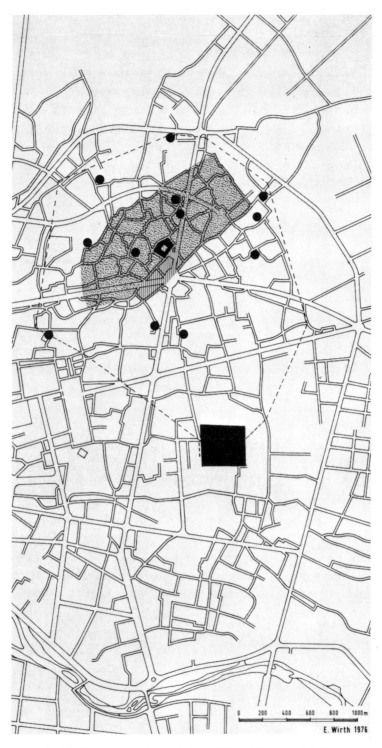

51. Buildings earlier than 1500 A.D. in Isfahan

commercial importance and cosmopolitan flair the literary sources bear witness.[50] In addition to these, small bazaars developed near the city gates. And along the axes there were linear bazaars as well. In one of them a traveler of the first half of the eleventh century saw no fewer than fifty caravansarais.[51] Around the administrative, religious, intellectual, and commercial center at the old *maidān* and the main axes of intra-urban communication there were the residential quarters with their sub-centers and secondary religious buildings. The latter, which were built Ill. 51 before 1500, are still preserved, and are indicated on Ill. 51.

These buildings are too few in number to enable us to draw conclusions that would go beyond those already made. The only point that their location in or near the original Yahūdiyya underlines is that here, north of the old *maidān,* was the nucleus of the city. With its twisted lanes, its high building density, and small lots, it resisted even the most trying periods of crisis.

3.7. Conclusion

The change of the political conditions in Iran after the decline of the Great Saljūq empire in the middle of the twelfth century deprived Isfahan of its function as capital city and dealt a severe blow to its economy which was heavily dependent on long-distance trade. In 1244 the city was captured by the Mongols. In Mongol times, Isfahan was a provincial capital, and obviously its economy was still prosperous, albeit more modest than under the Saljūqs. After the decline of the Mongol state in the second half of the fourteenth century, the Iranian Muẓaffarids, who had brought almost all of southern Iran under their control, ruled over Isfahan.

The year 1387 marks the end of an almost 800-year-long period of prosperity for Isfahan in Islamic times. In this year, Tīmūr conquered the city and ordered his soldiers to sack it. Many of the inhabitants were killed on that occasion. In 1414 a second sacking took place, and in 1474 Isfahan was reported to have had only about 50,000 inhabitants.[52]

4. THE DEVELOPMENT OF ISFAHAN UP TO 1700

4.1. Shāh Ismāʿīl and Shāh Tahmāsp

During the rise of the Ṣafavid state in the beginning of the sixteenth century, Isfahan was rebuilt by the first two *shāhs* of this dynasty, Ismāʿīl (1502-1524) and Tahmāsp (1524-1576). These two Ṣafavids integrated their buildings into the medieval plan of Isfahan. Their main concern

82

seems to have been the reconstruction and embellishment of the old *maidān*. Here they had erected no fewer than five buildings, one *madrasa* and one caravansarai, [53] most probably the predecessors of the *Madrasa* and Caravansarai Kāsah-Garān [54] on the northeast side of the square, the shrine Hārūn Vilāyat [55] opposite on the southwest side, the 'Alī Mosque [56] on the southeast corner of the *maidān*, and one caravansarai [57] north of it. In addition to this, these two rulers built two mosques, one *madrasa*, and one *ḥammām* along the road going from the *maidān* in a southwestern direction. Also a group of at least four caravansarais between the two mosques was most probably built in the time of these two rulers. [58]

4.2. Shāh 'Abbās I: *Maidān-i Shāh*

In the winter of 1597 Shāh 'Abbās I, *shāh* of Iran since 1587, decided to transfer his capital from Qazvin in northwestern Iran to Isfahan. This decision brought Isfahan in the course of only a few years to the highest point of its development and made it a capital of intercontinental importance, where envoys and merchants from Europe met those from the Far East.

In a very short period 'Abbās and his advisers seem to have laid out their basic concepts of how to rebuild and enlarge the city. Their plans directed the development of Isfahan along new paths and are comparable in their extent only with the foundation of the early Islamic city of Isfahan in the eighth century.

Unlike the sultans who had earlier ruled from Isfahan, and who had sometimes lived in the old city, 'Abbās decided not to live in the old city at all. He built his court on the southwestern edge of the city of those days. In this he followed trends known already in the Saljūq period, that is, to built royal compounds near the river. [59] 'Abbās went further, however, and created a new religious and economic center at the fringe of the sixteenth-century city. He thus forced further development of Isfahan into new directions.

The nucleus of 'Abbās' planning was once again a *maidān*, since this Ill. 52 was the ideal layout to unify the most important functions of a city as the administrative, religious, intellectual, and economic center. However, what had been developed at the old *maidān* in the course of the centuries was now recreated in a planned way, whereby the spatial distribution of buildings followed a considered organizational scheme.

Let us recall the features of the old *maidān*. The ratio between the length and width was about 3 to 1. Lanes through the bazaars run around it. The main thoroughfare through the bazaar was tangential to

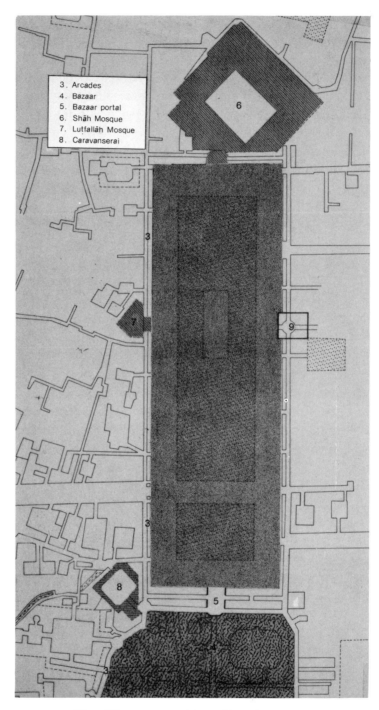

3. Arcades
4. Bazaar
5. Bazaar portal
6. Shāh Mosque
7. Lutfallāh Mosque
8. Caravanserai

52.   The new *maidān* of Isfahan

it. Bazaars were situated at its narrow sides. Near the royal bazaar, the *Qaiṣariyyah,* there was the *Naqqārah-Khānah,* the royal music pavilion, where at certain hours of the day trumpets were sounded and drums were beaten as part of the royal ceremony. The Friday Mosque was adjacent to this square. Next to it were other mosques, and *madrasas.* In addition to this, there was a royal palace at the *maidān.*

If we now look at the map of the new Ṣafavid *Maidān-i Shāh,* we can still locate all the elements of the old *maidān,* although the buildings are placed differently. In addition the *maidān* of the seventeenth century was Ill. 53 covered with sand, and at almost all times there were tents on it under which trade was carried on. On Fridays there was a weekly market for the village population from the surrounding countryside. At the two extremities of the square there stood posts because it served as a polo field from time to time as well. Trees lined the square, as they still do, and in front of the trees there ran a canal.

Behind the arcades running all around the *maidān* there were, in the east, west, and south, bazaar lanes with shops and workshops. The assortment of goods sold here, especially in the west, was aimed at satisfying the needs of the court. Jewels, gold, and silver objects, the work of silversmiths of Venice and Nuremberg, fine leather goods, and riding gear were offered for sale here. On the southern side, book dealers, book binders, stationers, trunk makers, and saddlers had their shops and workshops. On the eastern side there were the shops of various handicrafts. The northern edge of the square was lined with coffee houses whose upper floors were used as hostels and brothels.[60]

In four places, in the middle of the south and north sides and on the east and west sides slightly off the center towards the south, showy portals break the continuity of the facades. The portal on the south side leads into the Shāh Mosque, the "new" Friday Mosque, as it was called in the Ill. 54 time of the Ṣafavids.[61] The construction of the building began under 'Abbās I and was completed in 1631.[62] At the east side of the *maidān* is the portal of another mosque, the Luṭfallāh Mosque. It was begun in 1602 Ill. 55 and finished in 1618.[63]

4.3. Palace Complex

Facing the Luṭfallāh Mosque, at the west side of the Maidān-i Shāh, stands the 'Alī Qāpū, the High Gate, the reception palace of 'Abbās I Ill. 56 and his successors. According to local tradition, the building was erected on the site of a Tīmūrid pavilion in which 'Abbās I lived before he made Isfahan his capital.[64]

In the seventeenth century the 'Alī Qāpū was the entrance to the wide Ill. 57

85

53.   View of the new *maidān* of Isfahan

palace area which was adjacent to the *maidān* on the west. It extended westward as far as the Chahār-Bāgh boulevard. In this palace area there were kitchens, storage sheds, chicken houses, harem buildings, the private living quarters of the royal family, and pavilions in large parks which 'Abbās I and his successors had built. European travelers of the seventeenth century provide us with detailed descriptions of these pavilions.[65] Two of these pavilions are preserved, the Chihal-Sutūn[66] and the Hasht-Bihisht.[67]

West and south of the royal palace area on both sides of the Chahār-Bāgh and at the river as well there were mansions of the courtiers, whom 'Abbās I had ordered to build in that location. The Chahār-Bāgh, which crosses the governmental district, leads to one of the most beautiful bridges in the world, the 'Alī-Vardī-Khān Bridge. Its builder, 'Alī Vardī Khān, was one of the closest associates of Shah 'Abbās I.[68] Beyond this bridge, the Charār-Bāgh led to an enormous royal country residence, the Ill. 58 Hazār Jarīb. Located on rising terrain, Hazār Jarīb formed an impressive background for the Chahār-Bāgh to the south.[69]

Around 1700 Shāh Sultān Ḥusain, the last ruling Ṣafavid, built to the

86

54.　Portal of the Shāh Mosque of Isfahan

west of Hazār Jarīb another large palace garden complex, Faraḥ-Abād.[70] Both of these complexes have since disappeared.

'Abbās I ordered the building of the settlement of New Julfah, also to the south of the Zāyanda Rūd. Here he settled Armenians from Julfāh, and other parts of Armenia. 'Abbās transferred these people for both strategic and economic reasons. He wanted to create a belt of burned earth in the northwest of his empire in order to protect it against the Ottomans. However, 'Abbās was conscious of the industriousness and mercantile skills of the Armenians and he wanted them to contribute to the economic vitality of the city. (Eventually trade with Europe was almost exclusively conducted by the Armenians.)[71]

4.4. Bazaar North of the New *Maidān*

The bazaar north of the *maidān* is located to the south of the area where the pre-Ṣafavid and the Ṣafavid city impinge on each other. The monumental portal of this bazaar looks very much like the portal of the Shāh Mosque opposite it at the south end of the Maidān-i Shāh.[72] In Ṣafavid times it had a slightly different appearance, however. There were

Ill. 59

55.   Portal of the Luṭfallāh-Mosque of Isfahan

galleries on both sides, the *naqqārah-khānah* or the royal music pavilion, where, as a traveler of the seventeenth century wrote: "every evening at sunset and midnight many people play trumpets and big drums and some kind of exotic trumpets. This produces an awful noise. This music has nothing lovely in it, and only in comparison with a tocsin it might please." [73] Through the portal one enters a two-storied bazaar lane, the

Ill. 60 *Qaiṣariyyah.* This was the royal monopoly market in which, in the seventeenth century, fine fabrics were sold. In the middle of this lane there is a high dome. Underneath the dome to the right is the royal mint, while to the left one enters the shah's caravansarai which is today in poor condition.

This largest caravansarai of the city had a total of 140 rooms of different sizes on two floors. At the end of the seventeenth century cloth merchants from Tabriz, Qazvin, Ardabil, and India used the ground-floor rooms. On the upper floor jewelers, goldsmiths, and engravers had their shops and workshops.

North of the shah's caravansarai there is a similar caravansarai now in

56. The 'Alī Qāpū in Isfahan

even worse condition than the first. The area east of these caravansarais is
divided into squares by a system of bazaar lanes which intersect under
high domes, the *Chahār-sū.*

Although a great deal of rebuilding and restoration has taken place
since Ṣafavid times, we can still detect the master plan of the time of
'Abbās I. More, we can precisely distinguish that part of the bazaar
which belongs to the plan of 'Abbās I, a distinction which enables us to
delimit the building area of the times before 'Abbās I. The original plan
for the bazaar included two parallel roads running north and south
which intersected with three running east and west. In the squares
shaped by these lanes there were caravansarais, as there are today. Lane
120, now used as a bazaar, originally served to provide both the royal
mint and the Ḥammām-i Shāh, the "Shah's Bath," with fuel and other
materials. This system of bazaar lanes was connected with an original
south axis of the city at four points.

North of this bazaar which, as a whole, was called the *Qaiṣariyyah* in the
seventeenth century, there was a hospital, and next to it a caravansarai.

89

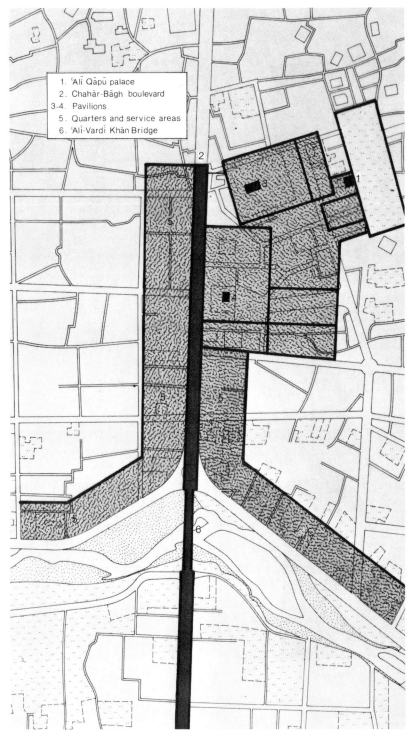

1. ʿAlī Qāpū palace
2. Chahār-Bāgh boulevard
3-4. Pavilions
5. Quarters and service areas
6. ʿAlī-Vardī Khān Bridge

57. The palace area of Isfahan

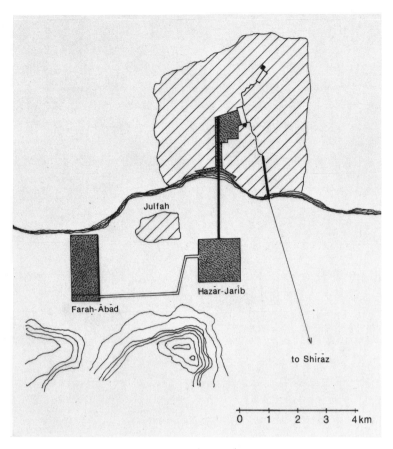

58. Isfahan and Julfah

which 'Abbās I had founded with the purpose of providing funds for the hospital. Both structures have since disappeared.

Further to the north, an emir of 'Abbās I, Jārchī-Bāshī, built a mosque and a caravansarai. They are built following the orientation of the second street scheme, which goes back to the early Middle Ages.[74] Street 209 is the old west axis of the city. Here the portal of a tenth-century mosque is preserved.[75] Only about 150 meters northeast of the caravansarai of Jārchī-Bāshī there is a mosque built in the time of Shāh Tahmāsp. All of this is clear evidence that here we are in the built-up area that existed in the period before 'Abbās I.

The plan originating from Maidān-i Shāh and the older pattern interfere with each other south of building 201, since caravansarai 199 was already built congruent with the orientation of the Maidān-i Shāh.

91

59.   The portal of the *Qaisariyyah*-bazaar of Isfahan

4.5. Bi-Polarity Old-New *Maidān*

The layout of the roads in the Maidān-i Shāh characterize the third of the older street patterns, the Ṣafavid, that we can detect in Isfahan. We find it as well in the southeastern sector of the city, in the area which we know was destroyed in pre-Ṣafavid times. Since the Ṣafavid street pattern is also predominant west of the old *maidān,* we may suppose that here too there was widespread destruction in the pre-Ṣafavid period. The overlapping of the three street plans can be observed in the entire bazaar area. Up to the intersection north of the buildings of Jārchī-Bāshī, the first two street patterns are apparent. In the north-south direction, the first and in the east-west direction, the second pattern dominates. Here in this area is the contact point between the fields of gravity of the old and the new *maidān*. The new *maidān* was not able to achieve such prominence that it became the sole urban center of Isfahan. This was due, above all, to the fact that the old Friday Mosque continued to be, in spite of the new Friday Mosque on the new *maidān*, the most important mosque of the city, attracting crowds of people to the area of the old *maidān*.

The buildings that were constructed in between the old and the new *maidān* show this bi-polarity [76] which was not at all what 'Abbās I had

60. Map of the southern part of the bazaar of Isfahan

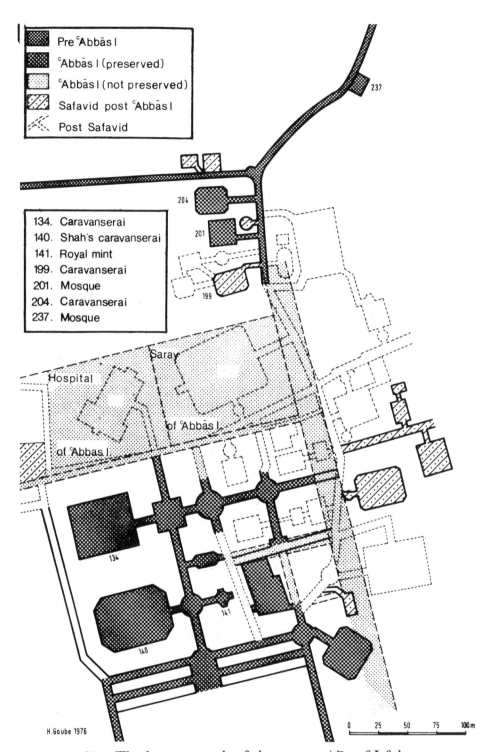

Legend:

- Pre ᶜAbbās I
- ᶜAbbās I (preserved)
- ᶜAbbās I (not preserved)
- Safavid post ᶜAbbās I
- Post Safavid

134. Caravanserai
140. Shah's caravanserai
141. Royal mint
199. Caravanserai
201. Mosque
204. Caravanserai
237. Mosque

Saray
Hospital
of ᶜAbbās I
of ᶜAbbās I

H. Gaube 1976

0   25   50   75   100 m

61. The bazaar north of the new *maidān* of Isfahan

intended, as contemporary sources witness. 'Abbās I's intention was to direct, if possible, all commercial activity from the old to the new *maidān* because he derived profits from the shops and caravansarais he had built there.[77]

It is fortunate that this decisive transfer of gravity did not occur, because this bi-polarity (between the old *maidān* and the new *maidān*) led to an organic and stable amalgamation of the Ṣafavid new city with the pre-Ṣafavid old city. The new urban unit was able to weather even a crisis as severe as the one after 1722 when the Afghans captured Isfahan. Due to this bi-polarity, the bazaar of Isfahan developed laterally and now lies like a bridge between the old and new *maidān*.

The result of the interference of these two fields of gravity is that in the areas of the first and second street patterns, the third, with its particular 346° street-orientation, forces itself into them. This 346° pattern is our next and last concern.

4.6. Ṣafavid Street Pattern

To ask the question where it originated is to raise the controversial question of why the Maidān-i Shāh has its strange orientation which is followed by the over-all Ṣafavid street pattern. The question we have to ask may be formulated as follows: Was the decision to orientate the Maidān-i Shāh in this way reached without the pressure of external forces or was it predetermined by the presence of already existing streets and structures?

That the decision was reached without pressure of external forces might be argued on the basis of the enormous area covered by the Maidān-i Shāh planning which was not restricted only to the *maidān* and the bazaar adjacent to it but continued far to the west and north. In addition to this, esthetic considerations have been advanced as arguments.[78]

It is also surprising that the Maidān-i Shāh has almost the same orientation as the large terrace at Persepolis which most likely was aligned according to astronomical calculations.

Against the free choice of a 346° orientation for the Maidān-i Shāh, some have advanced the argument of a pre-Ṣafavid pattern, i.e., garden limits, and *kūchahs*, small lanes that run around them, which 'Abbās I had to tolerate.[79] There may be some truth in this, but gardens and *kūchahs* certainly would not have hindered 'Abbās I from giving his *maidān* another orientation had he so chosen. What actually hindered 'Abbās was the pre-Ṣafavid south axis of the city that ran parallel to the Maidān-i Shāh. It was the busiest axis of Isfahan. Along this artery

Ill. 45

95

flowed all the traffic to and from the south, especially to Shiraz. Before 'Abbās I's time the bazaar stretched far to the south along this axis in the direction of Maidān-i Shāh. This axis ran south of the Darvāzah-i Ashraf, the old southwest gate, which most probably marked the limit of the medieval built-up area, in a straight line about 100 meters east of the Maidān-i Shāh, through the gardens to a predecessor of the Khvājū bridge. On this axis the new south gate, the Darvāzah-i Ḥasan-Abād was built.[80]

.That this is not just an idle theory is demonstrated by the present course of the south axis. North of the Maidān-i Shāh its integration into the *Qaiṣariyyah* complex looks entangled and artificial. A thorough study of the architecture of this area reveals that the connection between the south axis and the *Qaiṣariyyah* complex was frequently reshaped.[81]

South of the *maidān*, the south axis passes by a building, the Imāmzādah Aḥmad, in which a Saljūq inscription has been immured.[82] This is a strong indication that the axis passed here already in pre-Ṣafavid times.

The Bāzārchah Maqṣūd at the southeast corner of the Maidān-i Shāh, finally, built in the time of Shāh 'Abbās I, is clear evidence that the south axis passed east of the Maidān-i Shāh. Its only purpose could have been to connect the *maidān* with the south axis. A similar connection must have existed at the northeast corner of the Maidān-i Shāh, otherwise the absolutely illogical and purposeless location of an early tīmchah north of the Madrasa 'Abdallāh cannot be explained.

NOTES

1. Cf. E. Wirth, "Die orientalische Stadt. Ein Uberlick aufgrund jüngerer Forschung zur materiellen Kultur," *Saeculum,* 26 (1975), 45-94, 83.

2. Ptolemy: *Geography,* VI, 2 and 4.

3. J. Marquart, *Erānšahr nach der Geographie des Ps. Moses Xorenac'i* (Abhandlungen der Königlichen Gesellschaft der Wissenschaften zu Göttingen, Phil.-hist. Kl. N.F. III, 2) (Berlin, 1901), 27-30.

4. J. Marquart, *loc. cit.*

5. R. Göbl, "Aufbau der Münzprägung," F. Altheim und R. Stiehl, *Ein asiatischer Staat* (Wiesbaden, 1954), 298 ff.

6. Cf. G. Le Strange, *The Lands of the Eastern Caliphate* (³London, 1966), 202-207.

7. Māfarrūkhī, Muffaddal b. Saʻd, *Kitāb mahāsin Iṣfahān,* (ed.) J. al-Ḥusainī (Tehran, 1312/1933).

8. Abū Nuʻaim, Ahmad b. 'Abdallāh, *Kitāb akhbār Iṣbahān,* (ed.) S. Dedering (Leiden, 1934).

9. Abū Nuʻaim, *op. cit.,* 15.

10. Abū Nuʻaim, *loc. cit.*

11. L. Golombek, "Urban patterns in pre-Safavid Isfahan," *Iranian Studies,* 7 (1974), 18-44, 23. See also Ibn al-Faqīh, Aḥmad b. Muhammad, *Kitāb al-buldān,* (ed.) M. de Goeje (Leiden, 1885), 262. That Jayy originally was round is said by Ibn Rustah, Aḥmad b. 'Umar, *al-A'lāq an-nafīsa,* (ed.) M. de Goeje (Leiden, 1892), 160.

12. Abū Nu'aim, *loc. cit.*

13. Abū Nu'aim, *op. cit.,* 16.

14. Ibn Rustah, *op. cit.,* 161.

15. Ibn al-Nadīm, Muhammad b. Abī Ya'qūb, *Kitāb al-fihrist,* (ed.) G.L. Flügel (Leipzig, 1871-1872), 240.

16. Abū Nu'aim, *op. cit.,* 15.

17. Māfarrūkhī, *op. cit.,* 92.

18. Māfarrūkhī, *op. cit.,* 93.

19. Māfarrūkhī, *op. cit.,* 42.

20. Abū Nu'aim, *op. cit.,* 16.

21. L. Golombek, *op. cit.,* 24.

22. Abū Nu'aim, *op. cit.,* 16.

23. Cf. E. Reitemeyer, *Die Städtegründungen der Araber im Islam nach den arabischen Historikern und Geographen* (München, 1912).

24. Abū Nu'aim, *op. cit.,* 17.

25. J. Walker, *A Catalogue of the Arab-Byzantine and Post-Reform Umaiyad Coins* (London, 1956), LX f.; S. Lane-Poole, *Catalogue of the Oriental Coins in the British Museum,* I (London, 1875), 227-247.

26. G. Le Strange, *loc. cit.*

27. Cf. H. Gaube and E. Wirth, *Der Bazar von Isfahan* (Beihefte zum Tübinger Atlas des Vorderen Orients, Reihe B, Nr. 22) (Wiesbaden, 1978).

28. A. Godard, "Historique du Masdjid-é Djum'a Isfahan," *Athār-é Irān,* 1 (1936), 213-282; E. Galdieri, *Isfahān: Masǧid-i Gum'a. Restorations,* I, 1 and I, 2 (Rome, 1972-1973).

29. H. Gaube and E. Wirth, *op. cit.*

30. L. Hunarfar, *Ganjīnah-yi āsār-i tārīkhī-yi Isfahān* (Isfahan, 1344/1966), 652-656.

31. H. Gaube and E. Wirth, *op. cit.*

32. A. Godard, "Isfahān," *Athār-é Irān,* 2 (1937), 6-176, 63-69; L. Hunarfar, *op. cit.* 320-369.

33. A. Godard, *op. cit.,* 69-72; L. Hunarfar, *op. cit.,* 369-379.

34. J. Chardin, *Voyages en Perse et autres lieux de l'Orient,* vol. 8 (Amsterdam, 1711), 146. See also A. Godard, *op. cit.,* 14.

35. E. Herzfeld (ed. G. Walser), *The Persian Empire* (Wiesbaden, 1968), 22f.

36. Yāqūt, Ya'qūb b. 'Abdallāh, *Mu'jam al-buldān,* (ed.) G. Wüstenfeld (Leipzig, 1866-1873), IV, 713.

37. See above p.

38. E. Herzfeld, *Inscriptions et monuments d'Alep* (CIA, 2me partie: Syrie du nord) (Cairo 1955), 19f.

39. E. Herzfeld, *loc. cit.*

40. Abū Nu'aim, *op. cit.,* 16.

41. A. Godard, *op. cit.,* 13 f.

42. E. Kaempfer, *Amoenitatum exoticarum politico-physico-medicarum fasciculi V* (Lemgo, 1712), 169.

43. C.f. the lithographed map of Isfahan compiled for Riżā-Khān in 1302/1924, and H. Gaube and E. Wirth, *op. cit.*

44. Nāsir-i Khusrau, Abū Mu'īn, *Safarnāmah,* (ed.) M. Dabīrsiyāqī (Tehran, 1344/1966), 122.

45. E.F. Schmidt, *Flights over Ancient Cities of Iran* (Chicago, 1940), pl. 27. For the map cf. n. 43.

46. J. Chardin, *op. cit.,* 146.

47. e.g. Māfarrūkhī, *op. cit.,* 83; Yāqūt, op. cit., I, 677.

48. Māfarrūkhī, *op. cit.,* 53-56

49. J. Thévenot, *Des Herrn Thévenot's Reisen in Europa, Asien und Africa* (Frankfurt, 1693), 119.

50. Māfarrūkhī, *op. cit.,* 84; Muqaddasī, Muhammad b. Ahmad, *Kitāb ahsan at-taqāsīm fi ma'rifat al-aqālim,* (ed.) M. de Goeje (Leiden, 1906), 388.

51. Nāsir-i Khusrau, *loc. cit.*

52. The outlines of the history of Isfahan are given by A.K.S. Lambton, *EI²*, IV, 97-105

53. J. Chardin, *op. cit.*, 146.

54. Cf. H. Gaube and E. Wirth, *op. cit.*, nos. 360 and 361.

55. Cf. n. 32.

56. Cf. n. 33.

57. H. Gaube and E. Wirth, *op. cit.*, no. 287.

58. H. Gaube and E. Wirth, *op. cit.*, nos. 237, 260-262 and 267.

59. Māfarrūkhī, *op. cit.*, 53-56.

60. The best description of the *Maidān-i Shāh* in the seventeenth century are J. Chardin, *op. cit.*, 43-50; C. de Bruin, *Reizen over Moskovie door Persie en Indie* (Amsterdam, 1714), 147 f.; A. Olearius, *Vermehrte Moscowitische und Persianische Reisebeschreibung* (Schleswig, 1656), 554-558; J. B. Tavernier, *Les six voyages de Jean Baptiste Tavernier, en Perse, et aux Indes* (Paris, 1679), I, 442-447.

61. Iskandar Munshī, *Tārīkh-i ʿālam ārā-yi ʿAbbāsī*, (ed.) I. Afshār (Tehran, 1334-1335/1956-1958), 831.

62. A. Godard, *op. cit.*, 107-116; L. Hunarfar, *op. cit.*, 427-464.

63. A. Godard, *op. cit.*, 96-99; L. Hunarfar, *op. cit.*, 401-415.

64. A. Godard, *op. cit.*, 80-88; L. Hunarfar, *op. cit.*, 416-426.

65. E.g. J. Chardin, *op. cit.*, 68-83.

66. A. Godard, *op. cit.*, 116-120; L. Hunarfar, *op. cit.*, 457-474.

67. A. Godard, *op. cit.*, 147-149; L. Hunarfar: *op. cit.*, 487; I. Luschey-Schmeisser, *The pictorial title cycle of Hašt Behešt in Isfahan and its iconographic tradition* (IsMEO Reports and Memoirs 14) (Rome 1978).

68. A. Godard, *op. cit.*, 95 f.

69. E. E. Beaudouin, "Ispahan sous les grands chahs (XVIIᵉ siècle)," *Urbanisme*, II, 10 (1933), 1-47, 32-34; L. Hunarfar, *op. cit.*, 489-493.

70. E. E. Beaudouin, *op. cit.*, 34-36; L. Hunarfar, *op. cit.*, 722-725.

71. J. Carswell, *New Julfa* (Oxford, 1968).

72. Descriptions of all the bazaar buildings are to be found in H. Gaube and E. Wirth, *op. cit.*, part C; a functional and chronological map of the bazaar of Isfahan by the same authors was published in *Tübinger Atlas des Vorderen Orients (TAVO)*, map A IX, 9.4 (Wiesbaden, 1977).

73. J. Thévenot, *op. cit.*, 116.

74. See above

75. H. Gaube and E. Wirth, *op. cit.*, no. 222.

76. Cf. *TAVO*, map A IX, 9.4.

77. J. B. Tavernier, *op. cit.*, I, 441.

78. D. Wilbert, "Aspects of the Safavid ensemble of Isfahan," *Iranian Studies*, 7 (1974), 406-411.

79. L. Golombek, *op. cit.*, 31 f.

80. Cf. TAVO, map A IX, 9.4, 'H'.

81. H. Gaube and E. Wirth, *op. cit.*

82. L. Hunarfar, *op. cit.*, 669.

83. H. Gaube and E. Wirth, *op. cit.*, no. 30.

CHAPTER FOUR

Bam—A Provincial Center

1. INTRODUCTION

In comparison with Isfahan, with its more than 600,000 inhabitants, Bam, which in 1972 had 33,373 inhabitants, is very small.[1] Nevertheless, it is the largest settlement on the southern fringe of the Dasht-i Lūt, the southern of the two great Iranian deserts. Bam is the capital of a *shahristān*, and has had a long and checkered history.

Bam is situated on the road leading from western Iran to India and also connects the provinces of Fars and Kirman in the west and the province of Sistan in the east. In addition to this, Bam is connected via Jiruft to the south with the coast of the Persian Gulf.

1.1. Bam in the Tenth Century

Founded in pre-Islamic times, Bam had its heyday in the tenth century when it was one of the five provincial capitals of the land of Kirman.[2] Three large cities, Abārik, Rāyin, and Darzīn, and their hinterlands, all situated between Bam and Kirman, were administered from Bam.[3] Arab geographers of the tenth century, especially Muqaddasī, give us a good idea of the economic importance of Bam in that period. Muqaddasī writes: "Bam is an important provincial capital, pleasant and large. Its inhabitants are endowed with skill and dexterity. It is a marketplace attracting visitors from far away. Cloth produced here is known in many countries. The city is famous all over the Islamic world and a source of

99

pride for its country. Most of its inhabitants are weavers. Most of the garments exported from Bam are produced in a large village nearby. In the east and the west of the Islamic world these garments are considered to be very elegant. In addition to these, turbans, linen, tunics, and costly garments which are more sought after than those coming from Marv are produced in Bam." [4]

In this period, Bam, as a center of textile production, was integrated into an extensive network of long-distance trade that had been formed during the 'Abbāsid empire. Another Arab geographer, Ibn Ḥawqal, who wrote around 978, reports that the products of Bam were exported to Khurasan, Iraq, and Egypt. The same author further relates that the cotton from which these goods were produced was grown in the region of Bam.[5] (This remark suggests that in the Middle Ages there existed an extensive *qanāt* system around Bam, since the cotton plant requires considerable water for cultivation.)

1.2. History of Bam

The geographer Yāqūt, who wrote around 1225, describes Bam as a rich and bustling city.[6] Since he himself never came to Bam, it is quite possible that in his time conditions had already changed. Nevertheless, Bam shared the fate of other Iranian cities: Maladministration had brought on its decline. Thus, around 1300, the historian Rashīd al-Dīn wrote a letter to his son Maḥmūd, at that time the governor of Kirman, complaining about "the poverty-stricken conditions of the peasants of the province of Bam, ruined and in flight because of the extortion and violence practised by the military." [7]

Bam, which had a very small agrarian basis and thus depended on industry, could not prosper without the peasants of its hinterland. They maintained the extremely intricate and fragile *qanāt* system and they also cared for the oases. Evidence for this can be found some years after Rashīd al-Dīn in the geographical work of Ḥamdallāh Mustawfī, written in 1340. Ḥamdallāh reports no more about Bam than that there was a strong castle there.[8] One century later Bam had sunk to the level of a rural town, and no further mention is made of its industry.[9]

Due to its location, as the last southern bastion of western Iran toward the east, and its citadel, which already in the Middle Ages was considered to be impregnable, Bam was spared the fate of its medieval neighbors, Abārik, Darzīn, and Rāyin, which disappeared or were reduced to unimportant villages.

In the eighteenth century, Bam enjoyed a limited recovery, serving as the westernmost bastion of the Afghans. The Afghans were expelled in

100

1801 by the Persians.[10] Bam continued to flourish after the Persians made it one of the provisional capitals of the land of Kirman.[11]

In 1840, construction of the new city began southwest of the old city. And towards the end of the nineteenth and at the beginning of the twentieth century, Bam experienced a considerable economic boom. Many public buildings were erected, and its bazaar was extended. Around 1900 the city had about 13,000 inhabitants and was "the last commercial center in this part of Asia until Quetta [about 700 miles farther east] was reached." In addition to this, Bam owed its wealth to the fact that almost all of the valuable dye, henna, was produced in its district. And around 1900 Percy Sykes goes as far as to call the Bam of his time "a thriving center," with almost as many caravansarais—the best indication of the trade volume of a city—as Kirman.[12]

2. GEOGRAPHICAL LOCATION OF BAM

Northwest of Bam, in the direction of Kirman, are long stretches of hostile and arid highlands, dotted with cisterns and small caravansarais. Mahan is the only large settlement, about 36 kilometers from Kirman. It is a pilgrimage site for the shrine of the ṣūfī Nūr al-Dīn Niʻmatallāh, who died in 1441 in Mahan.[13] Otherwise, there are only small settlements between Bam and Kirman. Almost without exception they lie at the foothills of the mountains where streams and qanāts provide water for irrigation. Some of them, like Abārik, lie next to the sites of important medieval cities.

Southeast of Abārik, at a distance of only 30 kilometers from Bam, are the ruins of another medieval city of the province of Bam. Darzīn was very famous in the Middle Ages, and a poet of the twelfth century remarked: "We sat on the roof of the palace at Darzīn and looked at the number of villages touching each other and the fragrant scented trees . . . I swear that in the whole of Fars I have not seen such a spot!" [14]

East of Bam, there is only barren land, and immediately west of Zahidan, the modern capital of Sistan-Balujistan, the desert begins. Here the desert road is lined with ruined caravansarais, now no longer needed since the truck had replaced the camel. About 90 kilometers west of Bam, the Mīl-i Nādirī, built in 1073, stands isolated in the desert. This tower served, for centuries, as a landmark for the traveler who passed through the desert.[15] West of the Mīl-i Nādirī, near the Kūh-i Shīr mountains, there are a few small villages which are part of the hinterland of Bam. They are provided with water which is carried by qanāts from the foothills of the Kūh-i Shīr.

101

The villages have a number of features in common, which enable us to form a general idea of oasis agriculture. Let the village of Aḥmadiyyah, situated about 6 kilometers northeast of Bam, serve as an example.[16] The

Ill. 62   settlement and the irrigated fields are surrounded by a high mud wall, and the settlement itself lies in the southwestern corner. To the north and east, are fields crisscrossed with irrigation ditches in which henna, grapes, and alfalfa are cultivated.[17] In the southeast corner there are palm and citrus gardens. Under the trees, as a rule, alfalfa is sown. All this is surrounded by dry-farming land, on which wheat is grown in the years with sufficient rain.

Ill. 63   Aḥmadiyya is a typical farm workers' settlement. That is, the land belongs to an absentee landlord, and the farm workers cultivate the land for him. Since the houses for the farm workers are provided by the landlord, they are designed in an inexpensive barrack-like fashion around a courtyard that is entered from the south. The houses are situated on the east, south, and west sides. Stables are in the north. To the west of the large stable in the northeastern corner there are two corrals. They are directly accessible from the outside, and thus the herds do not have to cross the central courtyard every morning and evening.

About 100 kilometers southwest of Bam are the Kūh-i Shīr mountains. There is an abundance of water and many villages which are inhabited in the summer by people from Bam. They grow grain, which is essential to the survival of Bam.

Beside grain—more importantly—water also comes from the mountains south of Bam. It is the essential basis for the existence of both Bam and the villages of its hinterland. The water is brought to the settlements by way of *qanāts,* some of which are 20 kilometers and longer. Oasis agriculture, typical for this region, is made possible by these *qanāts.* Twenty-five *qanāts* alone supply Bam with water, providing its agro-economic basis.[18]

3. PRESENT-DAY BAM

More important than agriculture—in which (1970) nevertheless 17 percent of the gainfully employed population of Bam works—is Bam's urban function as the administrative and economic center of a vast hinterland.

More than 40 government offices, three hospitals, and 25 schools with about 7000 pupils, indicate Bam's importance as the administrative center. There are 550 shops devoted to wholesale and retail trade which prove the economic importance of the city. They are concentrated in the

102

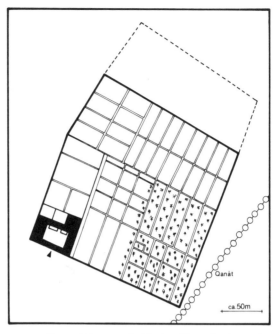

62.   The village of Aḥmadiyyah (map)

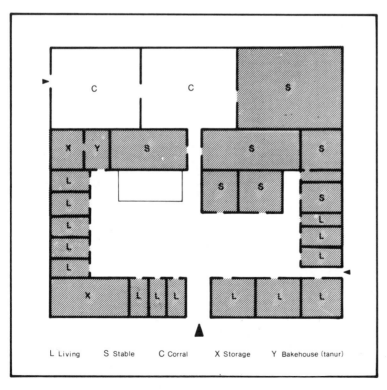

L Living   S Stable   C Corral   X Storage   Y Bakehouse (tanur)

63.   The village of Aḥmadiyyah (plan)

bazaar and in the area around or near the intersection of the two modern main streets. However, merchants have moved out of the bazaar into shops along the modern streets, due to the fact that the bazaar had lost its function as the main axis of the city. The two modern main streets have now acquired this function. The stream of pedestrians once flowing east-west through the bazaar, was detoured to the south and the west. Thus, the shops in the eastern part of the bazaar lost the basis for their existence and were abandoned. Even in the western part of the bazaar, which is very close to the modern main axis of the city, there are many vacant shops.[19]

In this general structural change Bam resembles a number of other Iranian cities of similar size, in which modern through streets have caused widespread abandonment of the bazaars. Bam's high proportion of garden land within the city, which is typical for oasis cities, does not distinguish this city from a number of other cities in Iran. Save for its old city, Bam would not merit being discussed next to Herat and Isfahan.

4. THE OLD CITY OF BAM

Ill. 64

In Bam, better than anywhere else in Iran, we can get a clear idea of a traditional small Iranian Islamic city. The old city of Bam is no longer inhabited, but it is preserved to such an extent that we easily can understand the original functions and features of the buildings. That is, unlike Herat and Isfahan, where the cycle of construction, abandonment, dilapidation or demolition, and reconstruction was never interrupted, here in Bam the conditions of an Islamic city as they were more than a hundred years ago are preserved. Here, some of the individual elements of the Islamic Iranian city can be studied.

4.1. Historical Topography of Bam

Before we begin our investigation, a bit of historical topography may prove useful. Let us see what we can learn about the form and extension of medieval Bam, and then follow the development of the city up to the present.

Very little has been written about medieval Bam.[20] Most of it is confused and incorrect because the brief descriptions of Bam by the medieval Arab geographers were misunderstood by Schwartz [21] and Le Strange, [22] the authors of the two standard works on medieval Persian geography.

Iṣṭakhrī [23] and Ibn Ḥawqal [24] write in their geographies, which were

104

64.   Aerial view of the old city of Bam

compiled around 951 and 971 respectively: "[Bam] has a famous *qal'a* [which is generally translated as 'citadel'] which lays in the city [the Arabic word used here is *madīna*]. In the city of Bam there are three Friday Mosques, the Khārijit's Mosque, the Mosque in the bazaar of the batiste merchants and the Friday Mosque in the *qal'a.*"

Almost anyone reading the Arab original of the quoted lines would translate *"qal'a"* as "citadel" and conclude that Bam had a citadel in which there was a Friday Mosque. Influenced by such an interpretation, the more precise description of Bam by Muqaddasī, written around 985, can easily be misunderstood or misinterpreted at a decisive point.[25] Muqaddasī calls Bam a flourishing provincial capital *(qaṣba)* and uses at another place the word *balad* for the city in general. This *qaṣba/balad* was dominated by a citadel for which Muqaddasī uses the word *ḥiṣn*. In the center of the city, *qaṣba* or *balad,* there was, according to Muqaddasī, the *qal'a* in which there was the Friday Mosque and some of the bazaars. Muqaddasī mentions only one Friday Mosque as opposed to the three mentioned by Iṣṭakhrī and Ibn Ḥawqal.

Qal'a and *ḥiṣn* are here clearly distinguished and we must translate *ḥiṣn* as "citadel." *Qal'a* must, then, be something other than a citadel and should probably be translated as "circumvallated inner city," for which the anonymous Persian geographical work, the *Ḥudūd al-ʿālam,* gives the Persian equivalent *shahristān.*[26] Bam as a whole is called a *qaṣba* by Muqaddasī, according to its functions as administrative center, and *balad* as city in general.

From this we can derive the following schematic idea of medieval Bam. In the center of the city was the circumvallated inner city with bazaars and the Friday Mosque. Both were dominated by the citadel.

In addition to this Muqaddasī writes: "Through the city [*balad*] flows a *nahr.* First it flows along the periphery of the city, then it flows through the bazaar of the batiste merchants, reaching the inner city [*qal'a*] next, and after this it flows toward the gardens."

Important points of reference for a topographic interpretation of this information are the citadel (*ḥiṣn*), the inner city (*qal'a/shahristān*), and the *nahr.*

The present-day citadel is situated on the highest natural elevation around, which rises about 45 meters above the plain of Bam. At its foot one finds medieval sherds washed down from the citadel. There is no question that the present-day citadel lies on the site of the medieval citadel.

The present-day old city of Bam (without the secondary northwestern extension, to which I shall return later,) stands approximately 5 meters above the surrounding terrain. This elevation is not natural but it is the product of the accumulation of debris. This accumulation took place over a period of centuries. Thus, there is good reason to locate the medieval *qal'a*, that is, the circumvallated inner city, on the site of the present-day old city. In this *qal'a* there was a part of the bazaars (Muqaddasī uses the plural) and the Friday Mosque.

In analyzing the plan of the old city of Bam we can reach some conclusions. The nucleus of it is given by a rectangle about 425 meters long (east-west) and about 300 meters wide (north-south). The citadel is attached to this rectangle in the north. Between the citadel and the city's nucleus there is an open space. To this the northwestern quarter, which has a trapsoid-like shape, measuring about 175 meters square, was added later.

The rectangular nucleus is identical with the medieval *qal'a* or *shahristān*. It is divided into *insulae* by a system of lanes which run through it. These axes are roughly orientated to the cardinal points of the compass. There are three clearly distinguished roads running in south-northern direction (Ill. 66, A-C) and two running in east-western direction (Ill. 66, D and E). There were certainly two gates in the southern wall (the one used today, Ill. 66, 1, and a second, Ill. 66, 1, which led to the mosque). Most probably there were two more gates, one in the eastern and one in the western wall (Ill. 66, G and H).

In this general layout we discover a certain similarity with the *shahristāns* of Central Asian cities such as Khivah,[27] for example, which we have already compared with the *madīna* of Herat.[28] As in Herat, Khivah and Bukhara, the inner circumvallated city (*madīna, qal'a, shahristān*) of Bam was surrounded by an outer city. Thus this combination of a small inner city with an outer city (circumvalleted or not) can still be followed along a line which streches from the southern fringe of the Dasht-i Lūt to the region of Lake Aral. In such an extent and with such clearity, it is not detectible in the west of the two inner Iranian deserts and seems to be a mark of destinction of eastern Iranian cities.

On the basis of the present street network in the old city of Bam, we can locate with a high degree of certainty medieval bazaars. At that time the *qal'a* had at least four gates. So, we may suppose that the city had at least one east-west and one north-south axis, which were lined by shops and workshops. These two most probably lie under the present-day gate—*qal'a* and the most articulated east-west lane.

The present-day old city mosque testifies, by its dimensions, to better times. It is situated at the putative east-west axis of the medieval *qal'a*. Since we know that the old city of Bam was continuously inhabited from the Middle Ages to the nineteenth century, there is good reason to see in the old city mosque a successor of the medieval Friday Mosque.

The *nahr* of which Muqaddasī writes cannot be identical with the Rūd-i Pusht which flows some 100 meters north of the city. Its bed is more than 100 meters wide. This shows that during the rainy season an enormous quantity of water flows through its channel. This water, had it been allowed to flow through the city, would have caused great devastation every year.

In the north, the Nahr-i Shahr touches the old city. Like the Rūd-i Pusht, it dries up in summer. The word *nahr* in Persian denotes "canal," as opposed to *rūd* or *rūdkhānah* meaning "river." The Nahr-i Shahr, or a similar, somewhat more southerly flowing canal, are most likely the *nahr* of Muqaddasī.

Since the plain of Bam slopes slightly from west to east the current in the canal must have flowed in this direction. This means that the part of the city in which there was the batiste merchants' bazaar, and where, according to Iṣṭakhrī and Ibn Ḥaqal, one of the three Friday Mosques of Bam was situated, must have been located west of the present-day old city, because the water flowed through this part of the city before it reached the *qalʿa*. East of the circumvallated inner city, the water flowed towards the gardens. These gardens, however, were not directly adjacent to the inner city since Muqaddasī writes that the inner city was situated in the center of the unfortified city. Medieval shards which can be found east of the old city prove this conclusion.

Ill. 67 Thus medieval Bam was divided into

1. the small circumvallated inner city with bazaars and the Friday Mosque;
2. densely built-up but unfortified quarters with bazzars and mosques around it;
3. the farmland of the oasis dotted with houses.

In this Bam resembles pre-Tīmūrid Herat and other oasis cities.

The *qalʿa*, the old city, was the stable nucleus into which Bam would recede in periods of economic decline and general political instability, during the late and post medieval times. Its circumvallation was steadily strengthened through the eighteenth and nineteenth centuries. As a consequence of these works, slight changes in the course of the medieval walls could have taken place. Major alterations, however, were not made, since they would be visible in the relief of the city as it now appears.

Pottinger, who in 1810 visited Bam, describes the city walls as they appear today. He says: [The fortifications of Bam] "are now accounted beyond any comparison the most defensible in Persia. They have an elevated site, and at present consist of a very high and thick mud wall, a

108

deep, broad, and dry ditch, with six large bastions on each face, exclusive of those at the corners ... there is one gate between the two center bastions of the south face."[29]

In the middle of the nineteenth century, when the province of Kirman, under capable governors experienced a rapid economic growth, [30] the old city of Bam became too small for the growing population. To the southwest of it a new city arose which, around the end of the nineteenth century, had attracted the entire population of the old city. In this period Bam equalled Kirman in its economic importance.[31]

4.2. Conclusion

(After this digression into historical topography, we can see that in the Middle Ages the old city was furnished with a citadel, mosque, and bazaar which were essential for the performance of its urban functions as an administrative, religious, intellectual, and economic center. Even if, in the course of continuous strengthening of the fortifications during the eighteenth century and in the reduction of the number of gates to one, certain elements of medieval Bam became blurred, Under the new and certain elements of medieval Bam became blurred, under the new and changed circumstances a modified functional system developed which is as a model for an Islamic city, Bam provides a highly characteristic type due to the fact that here, in a tiny area, the essential urban institutions are united in a transparent arrangement which proves the theory which was laid out earlier on the location-determining forces at work inside the Islamic city. That is, the citadel lies inside the city walls but at the edge of the city. The connection between the gate and the citadel, the administrative center of Bam and its hinterland, became the main axis of intra-urban communication; it is, the bazaar. Not far from the end of this axis, at the foot of the citadel, there is a caravansarai. At the intersection of this north-south axis with the old east-west axis there is a square, a *maidān*, which fulfills both an economic function, as part of the bazaar, and a religious function as a *takyah*. At the old east-west axis there is the Friday Mosque. In its vicinity there are prestigious living quarters.)

5. A PHYSICAL DESCRIPTION OF THE OLD CITY OF BAM

Let us now take a closer look at the old city of Bam. This can easily be done by way of an imaginary promenade, on which we, like archeologists on a dig, can read the original functions of ruins on the basis of their present-day appearance and their location.

We start at the gate. A ramp leads to the first gate behind which there   Ill. 65 and 66,1

65.   The old city of Bam, view from the south

is an octagonal space with rooms for the guards. From there one enters the city through a second inner gate.

Ill. 68   If we then climb to the gate tower our eyes wander over the ruins which, now smoothed by the rains of many years, look as if they are about to melt. On the left one sees the inner face of the western city wall. Between this wall and the lane in the center there are residential quarters. The citadel towers over the whole city, and the north-south axis, the bazaar, leads from the gate to the citadel.

Ill. 66,5   The bazaar was originally vaulted. Shops line it on both sides. The shops consist of front rooms which open onto the bazaar and back rooms which were accessible through doors. The subdivision of the shops into front and back rooms is, in the Iranian bazaar—and in the bazaar in general—not the rule, but rather, it appears only in isolated cases, where there is enough space.

About 120 meters south of the gate the bazaar runs into the lane coming from the east. In this lane one can recognize one of the old thoroughfares. Here, a square, the *maidān/takyah* is located. It is

110

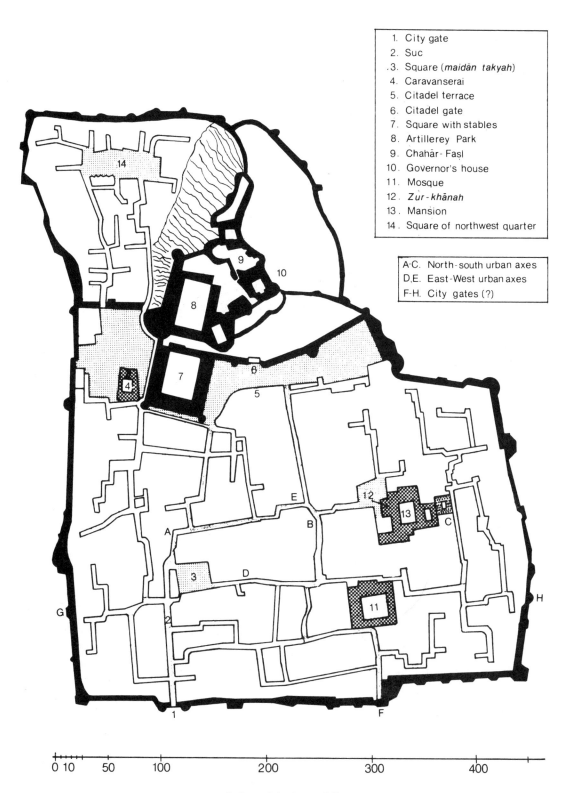

1. City gate
2. Suc
.3. Square (*maidān takyah*)
4. Caravanserai
5. Citadel terrace
6. Citadel gate
7. Square with stables
8. Artillerey Park
9. Chahār- Faṣl
10. Governor's house
11. Mosque
12. *Zur-khānah*
13. Mansion
14. Square of northwest quarter

A-C. North-south urban axes
D,E. East-West urban axes
F-H. City gates (?)

0 10 50 100 200 300 400

66. Map of the old city of Bam

111

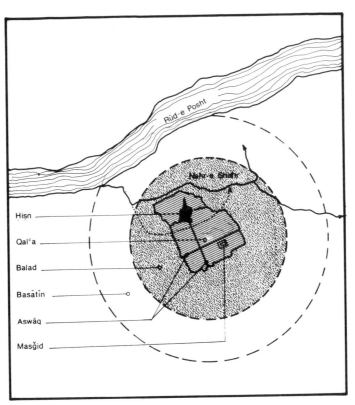

Rūd-e Posht

Nahr-e Shafr

Hiṣn

Qalᶜa

Balad

Basātin

Aswāq

Masǧid

67. Medieval Bam (scheme)

surrounded on all four sides by recesses and shops rising to two stories. This square resembles a large caravansarai.

During most of the year craftsmen worked here, and merchants transacted their business, much as they did at the *maidān* of Isfahan. It is possible that some trade also took place here. But, in the first third of the month of *Muḥarram,* the first month of the Muslim year, especially on the 10th of *Muḥarram,* a stage was constructed here and the *Taᶜziya,* the passion play of the Shiites, was performed. In this play, which is a suite of individual, only loosely connected tableaux, the Shiites evoke the martyrdom of Ḥusain, the grandson of the Prophet Muḥammad, at Karbala. The progress of the martyrdom, its prehistory and the prophecies of Ḥusain's death, some of them going back to Abraham and Moses, was enacted.[32]

Let us now go back to the bazaar and follow the north-south road to the citadel. Not far north of the *takyah* we come to an open space which is dominated by one of the towers of the citadel. In front of this tower we turn to the left and come to a wide space. Here a building which is

112

68.   The old city of Bam, view from the gate tower

closely connected organizationally with the bazaar, a caravansarai, is
situated. Behind the portal one enters a high *iwān* from which staircases
lead to the upper floor. The *iwān* opens onto a rectangular courtyard,
which is surrounded by buildings two stories high. The courtyard is
surrounded by rooms for foreign merchants. Because this caravansarai
was built at the foot of the citadel we can assume that it also served as a
customs office, where all goods entering the city were cleared. The open
space north and west of the building most probably served for keeping
pack animals.

Ill. 66,4, 70 and 71

If we return to the bazaar again we can see the gate of the citadel. In
front of it there is a huge square. At its south side, opposite the citadel
gate, is an elevated terrace. Here, presumably, the governor or his deputy
sat at times, heard complaints, and made decisions. Here too, most
probably, punishments were meted out and honors bestowed.

Ill. 66,5 and 72

Only high ranking visitors were allowed access to the citadel. Let us
now follow two of these visitors, Pottinger, who, in 1810 visited the
governor, and Sykes, who visited the citadel in 1895, when it was used
only for military purposes, while the seat of administration had already
been transferred to the new city. Sykes writes:

. . . ascending a steep incline in the rock, which has never been
smoother [but which is now], we passed through a strong gateway and

Ill. 66,6

113

69.   The *takyah* in the old city of Bam

Ill. 66,7 and 73

a 40-foot wall, which is built of sun-dried bricks, as indeed is the whole fortress. We then found ourselves facing a second and equally high wall, some 20 yards up the hillside, and, turning sharply to the left, approached the second gateway, a square surrounded by stables being below us as we moved along.

Ill. 66,8 and 74

A second equally steep incline, leading up to a similar gateway brought us to the Artillery Park where we saw some muzzle-loading field-guns mounted on unserviceable carriages; the date of one I remember, was A.H. 1254 (1838).

Ill. 66,9

A third and steeper passage led up from this square to a platform, on which is a well, which we calculated to be some 180 feet deep. A short flight of steps, and we reached the summit of the fort, a Chahar Fasl or Four Seasons, evidently constituting the Governor's quarters.[33]

Ill. 75

The Chahār-Faṣl is a favorite Iranian architectural type. It consists of four corner rooms which are connected to each other by vaults. The center is spanned by a dome. Open on all four sides, cool breezes constantly refresh those who happened to be there.

114

70. Caravansarai in Bam

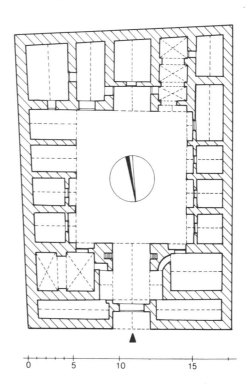

71. Caravansarai in Bam

0   5   10   15

72. Building opposite the citadel gate in Bam

Besides the Chahār-Faṣl, other buildings, of course, formed the residence of the governor. If we look from the Chahār-Faṣl to the southeast we see to the left an *īwān* with adjacent rooms and in the center a tower. In this tower most probably there was a windmill which the Persian historian Wazīrī, around 1860, refers to in his description of Bam.[34]

Behind the tower, farther to the east, there was the house of the governor, in which Pottinger was received in 1818. He writes:

The room we entered was a very handsome square one, with a recess and bow window on each side, the floor was covered with rich Persian carpets, and round the walls Numuds, or felts, for sitting upon. It was painted a pure white with gilt mouldings, and had altogether a very magnificent but not gaudy, effect.[35]

About fifty years after Pottinger's visit, the Persian historian Wazīrī gives a description of the citadel of Bam.[36] At that time there was only a

116

73. The citadel of Bam, stables

74. The citadel of Bam, barracks

75. The top of the citadel of Bam

76. The governor's house in the citadel of Bam

small garrison of about 100 foot soldiers, some artillery, who had two guns, fifty horses, and one commander.

Let us now return to the city. Coming from the citadel we turn south to the *takyah* and then east. Passing by plain high walls without windows, we soon see the minaret of the mosque. Originally, the mosque was built of mud bricks, as well as all the buildings of the city. (The north and south faces of the courtyard which are now covered with baked bricks, are the products of restoration works.) As with many mud-brick buildings, we face here the problems of dating, which cannot be done easily. On the sketch plan I have attempted to establish a rough subdivision of four building periods. I do not consider this chronology completely definitive since only thorough, precise and numerous measurements, combined with sondages, can provide precise results.

Ill. 77

Ill. 78

In the middle of the *qibla* side stand the side walls of a high *īwān*. This *īwān* doubtlessly is the oldest part of the structure. The thickness of its walls and the height of the *miḥrāb*—its upper part is visible above the roof of the built-in structure—isolate this *īwān* from the other, much lower parts of the building.

A small prayer hall was built adjacent to the *qibla-īwān* at the north side. In its stucco-decorated *miḥrāb* fragments of an inscription, dated 1164/1751, are preserved. This provides us with a *terminus ante quem* of 1751 for the great *īwān*. This means it was erected at the latest in the Ṣafavid period (seventeenth century), while its northern annex dates from the century in which Bam was mostly under Afghan rule.

Those parts of the mosque which lie east of the *īwān* facade follow a unified conception. The south-north axis of the courtyard is articulated by two wide but not high *īwāns*. East and west of these *īwāns* two-naved *riwāqs* line the courtyard. This part of the building is more recent than the *qibla-īwān* and the prayer hall in the northwest corner. But most probably it stands on an old foundation. As it is today, it dates back to the middle of the nineteenth century when the Afghans were expelled from Bam and the city started to prosper. At that time the *qibla-īwān* must have still been intact. Later, after the collapse of the *qibla-īwān* in and around it, some restoration work was done.

Although there is no material evidence to date the mosque in the old city of Bam farther back than the seventeenth century, we can assume that it stands at the site of the Friday Mosque mentioned by Muqaddasī and the other Arab geographers.

If we leave the mosque through its north gate and turn first to the west and then to the north, we reach another road which runs east and west, leading to a small square. There lies, incorporated into a huge mansion—at which we shall have a closer look later—the *zūr-khānah*. *Zūr-khānah*

119

77.   The Friday Mosque of the old city of Bam, view of the courtyard

Ill. 79   literally means "house of strength"; the *zūr-khānah* is the traditional Persian gymnasium.[37]

Ill. 80   Through an entrance *īwān* which is now collapsed, one enters a room shaped in the form of a cross, spanned with a dome in the center. The floor of the central portion of this room is lower than the floors of the four *īwāns* around it. Here, in the center is the *gaud* (pit), an area provided for physical exercises.

It does not appear accidental that our *zūr-khānah* is part of the architectural body of a large mansion. The *zūr-khānah* is situated at the northwestern corner of this complex, and we can presume that the master of this mansion understood how to use the members of the *zūr-khānah* fraternity, whom he obviously patronized, in Bam's city politics.

Ill. 66,13   The mansion to which the *zūr-khānah* is attached is typical, in the neighborhood north of the Great Mosque, of the size and architectural refinements of homes in Bam. At least a dozen similar houses can be

120

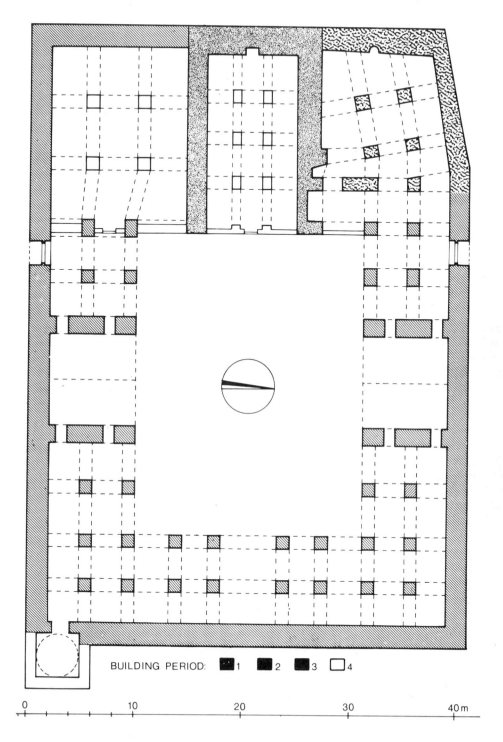

BUILDING PERIOD: ■1 ■2 ■3 □4

0   10   20   30   40 m

78. The Friday Mosque of the old city of Bam

121

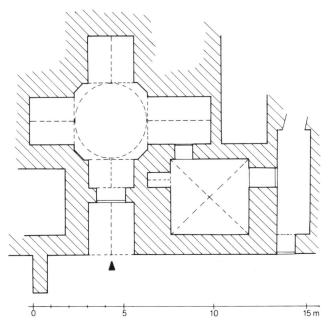

79. The *zūr-khānah* in the old city of Bam

found here. In the essentials of its plan, this mansion is a typical patrician
house of the Islamic Near East. Its main characteristics are the clear
division into a public part, in which the master receives his guests, and
into a private section which is reserved exclusively for the family. The
house has three entrances. The one from the east leads to the pantries
and servants' quarters. The one from the south leads to the private living
quarters, the harem. And the one from the west leads to the public part
of the building.

Ill. 81   Passing out of the *zūr-khānah*, we first direct our attention to the stables.
Behind the gate lies a large courtyard, with mangers on three sides.

The peculiarity of this house is, however, that adjacent to it we find
large stables on the south side of the courtyard. The roof of the stable
consists of six domes held by two massive pillars.

We may presume that the master of this mansion was one of those
merchants who knew how to exploit, for business purposes, the unique
geographical position of Bam between western Iran and the Indian
subcontinent.

Let us now go into the house through the east entrance. Behind the
door there is a rather narrow passage with a bench for people waiting to
Ill. 80,82 be received. At the end of the passage we enter the first courtyard.
Recesses in the walls decorate the eastern and western sides of the

122

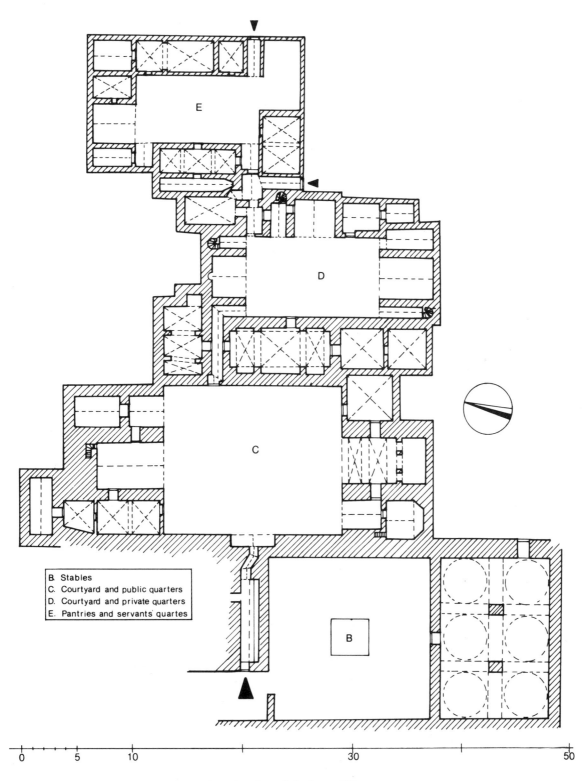

B. Stables
C. Courtyard and public quarters
D. Courtyard and private quarters
E. Pantries and servants' quartes

0   5   10   30   50

80. Mansion in the old city of Bam

123

81.   Mansion in the old city of Bam, stables

82.   Mansion in the old city of Bam, courtyard C

124

83.   Mansion in the old city of Bam, courtyard D

84.   Mansion in the old city of Bam, courtyard E

85.   View of the northwestern quarter of Bam

courtyard. In the center of its south and north sides there are high *īwāns*. These *īwāns* are connected by doors with lower adjacent rooms which have a second floor. Here in this first courtyard the master of the house received his visitors, served them tea (for this purpose there was a small tea kitchen in one of the side-rooms of the north *īwān*), and lodged them.

From this first courtyard a passage leads to another courtyard. Also, from this passage doors open into a kitchen and the furnace *(tanūr)* to the north and to the south one enters a large store room. At its end the passage makes a 90-degree bend to the private living section. The turn blocks this area from the view of the visitors entering the first courtyard.

The courtyard in the private section of the house is surrounded on three sides by *īwāns* and two-storied rooms. In the southeast corner of this courtyard a small door leads to a private *hammām*, and from the northeast corner of this courtyard a third passage leads to the pantry and servant's quarters, and to another entrance.

As opposed to the facades of the two first courtyards, which were decorated with recesses and mouldings, the facades of these parts are

126

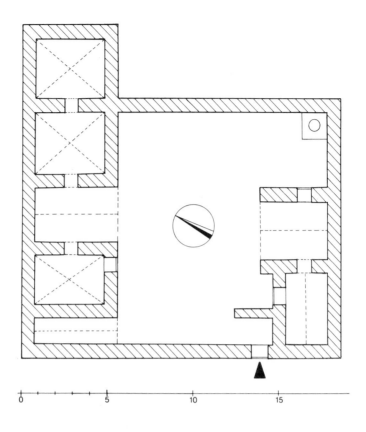

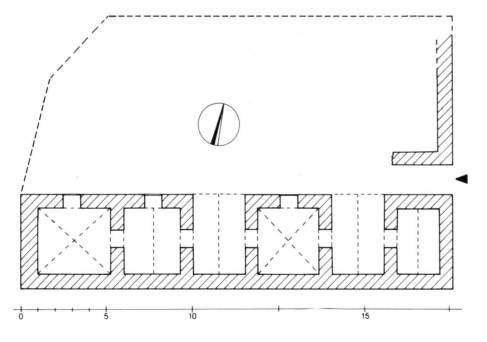

86, 87. Plan of a house in the northwestern quarter of Bam

88. View of a house in the northwestern quarter of Bam

89. House in Kirmania

plain. Here was the pantry; dishes and linen were washed and other household work was done; the servants also had their rooms here.

Finally, we turn to the northwestern section of the city. A wall separates this part of Bam from the rest of the city. This wall most probably is part of the medieval north city wall. In this wall there still stands a tower, projecting northward. Probably, this part of Bam is an extension of the city built after medieval times. The area is composed of small lots and a narrow system of lanes which meet at an open space in the center. The type of houses we find here is that of rural settlements. They are built with individual rooms that flank courtyards on one or two sides. Ill. 66, 14 and 85

Two houses may serve as examples. Both lie close to the north city wall. In the first house, on the south of the courtyard there is an *iwān*. To the west of it is a small room and to the east an open space with a *tanūr*. The living quarters proper are located at the north side of the courtyard facing the first group of rooms. Ill. 86

The other house has rooms only at the south side of the courtyard. In the north and west its courtyard touches the city wall. The house shows a surprising similarity with rural houses of Kirmania. Characteristics of this type of house, which are also popular in Kuhistan, are *iwāns* open to the courtyard and connected with side rooms. Such structures are always built with one *iwān* and one room on each side. If the family increases in number, or a son marries and decides to live with his parents, another unit, consisting of an *iwān* plus one or two rooms, is added. Ill. 87 and 88

Ill. 89

It is not easy to determine exactly who lived in the northwestern section of the city. Perhaps poor people or peasants lived here. As another possibility, an ethnic or religious minority may have. The first possibility is most unlikely. Poor people have always existed in a city. Their houses were integrated into the various neighborhoods as the city expanded. It is an established fact that in the traditional Islamic city rich and poor live side by side and not in isolated neighborhoods. Nor does it appear justified to claim that this northwestern section of Bam was the quarter of an ethnic or religious minority. Even if one thinks of Sunni Pashtūs who remained in Bam after the Afghans were expelled and Shiite Persians reconquered the city, or Zoroastrians, a number of whom still live in Bam, we should not connect these or other minorities with the northwestern quarter of the old city because this would presuppose that not only had they been discriminated against because of their religion, but were also forced to live in much worse social conditions than the rest of the population of Bam. We have no proof at all of such double discrimination. In many cases we observe the opposite, that is, minorities,

129

90. Map of Iran with the places mentioned in the book

130

because of the special strain placed on them, make greater efforts and their neighborhoods often look more prosperous than those of the majority.

There is only the third possibility left. Both the architectural style and historical evidence suggest that the northwestern quarter of Bam was inhabited by peasants. When, in the eighteenth century, Bam frequently changed hands and hordes of undisciplined soldiers and hostile tribesmen were the lords of the depopulated hinterland of Bam, the few surviving peasants could no longer live in the unfortified houses in the oases. They had no choice but to leave their villages and isolated homesteads and search for shelter within the walls of Bam. The resulting population growth most probably brought about the northwestern extension of the city. Here the peasants could, at least, save their lives, even if their fields and gardens remained exposed to plunderers and marauders.

At that time the only secure cultivated area around Bam lay north of the city in an area surrounded by strong walls.

NOTES

1. Most of the figures and information concerning modern Bam and its hinterland are based on: E. Ehlers, "Die Stadt Bam und ihr Oasen-Umland/ Zentraliran," *Erdkunde*, 29 (1975), 38-52.

2. Balādhurī, Ahmad b. Yahyā: *Kitāb futūh al-buldān*, (ed.) S. al-Munajjid (Cairo, n.d.), 482.

3. G. Le Strange, *The Lands of the Eastern Caliphate* (³London, 1966), 312 f.

4. Muqaddasī, Muhammad b. Ahmad: *Kitāb ahsan at-taqāsīm fī ma'rifat al-aqālīm*, (ed.) M. de Goeje (Leiden, 1906), 465.

5. Ibn Hawqal, Abū 'l-Qāsim b. Hasan, *Kitab surat al-ard* (Beirut, n.d.), 271.

6. Yāqūt, Ya'qūb b. 'Abdallāh, *Mu'jam al-buldān*, (ed.) F. Wüstenfeld (Leipzig, 1866-1873), I, 737.

7. J. A. Boyle (ed.), *The Saljuk and Mongol Periods (The Cambridge History of Iran)*, vol. 5 (Cambridge, 1968), 528.

8. Hamdallāh Mustawfī, Muhammad b. Nasr: *Nuzhat al-qulūb*, (ed.) M. Dabīrsiyāqi (Tehran, 1336/1958), 171.

9. For the period after Hamdallāh Mustawfī see J. Aubin, "Fragments historiques concernant Bam sous les Timurides et les Qara Qoyunlu," *Farhang-i Irān-zamīn* (Tehran, 1333/1955), 93-232.

10. G. N. Curzon, *Persia and the Persian Question* (²London, 1966), II, 253.

11. P. Sykes, *Ten Thousand Miles in Persia* (London 1902), 47: Wazīrī: *Jughrāfiyā-yi Kirmān* (ed.) I. B. Pārīzī (Tehran, 1353/1975), 92-102.

12. P. Sykes: *op. cit.*, 217.

13. Wazīrī: *op. cit.*, 82-84.

14. P. Sykes, *op. cit.*, 215.

131

15. P. Sykes, *op. cit.*, 418.
16. Cf. E. Ehlers, *op. cit.*, 41.
17. W. B. Fisher (ed.), *The Land of Iran (The Cambridge History of Iran*, vol. 1) (Cambridge, 1968), 100.
18. E. Ehlers, *op. cit.*, 43.
19. Cf. E. Ehlers, *op. cit.*, fig. 4.
20. Cf. L. Lockhard, "Bam," *EI* ², I. 1039-1040.
21. P. Schwarz, *Iran im Mittelalter* ·(²Hildersheim, 1969), 236-239.
22. G. Le Strange, *op. cit.*, 312 f.
23. Iṣṭakhrī, Ibrāhīm b. Muḥammad, *Kitāb masālik al-mamālik,* (ed.) M. al-Ḥīnī (Cairo, 1961), 99.
24. Ibn Ḥawqal, *loc. cit.*
25. Muqaddasī, *loc. cit.*

26. *Hudūd al-'ālam,* (ed.) M. Sutūdah (Tehran 1340/1962), 128.
27. W. A. Lavrov, *Gradostroitelnaja kultura srednei Asii* (Moscow, 1950), fig. 41.
28. See above
29. H. Pottinger, *Travels in Beloochistan and Sind* (London, 1816), 201.
30. H. Busse, "Kermān im 19. Jahrhundert nach der Geographie des Wazīrī," *Der Islam,* 50 (1973), 284-312.
31. P. Sykes, *op. cit.*, 350.
32. Cf. *EI* ¹, IV, *s.v.: Ta'zīya.*
33. P. Sykes, *op. cit.*, 218.
34. Wazīrī, *op. cit.*, 94.
35. H. Pottinger, *op. cit.*, 196.
36. Wazīrī, *op. cit.*, 92-94.
37. Cf. *EI* ¹, IV, *s.v.: Zūrkhāne.*